THE GIANT BK OF DIRTY LIMERICKS

THE GIANT BOOK OF DIRTY LIMERICKS

Over 1,000 Raunchy Rhymes

Compiled by
Rudy A. Swale

Ulysses Press

Published in the U.S. by:
ULYSSES PRESS
P.O. Box 3440
Berkeley, CA 94703
www.ulyssespress.com

First published in the U.K. in 2009 as *1000 Limericks You Could Never
Tell Your Mother* by Facts, Figures & Fun, an imprint of AAPPL Artists'
and Photographers' Press Ltd.

ISBN 978-1-56975-813-7
Library of Congress Control Number 2010925857

Printed in the United States by Bang Printing

10 9 8 7 6 5 4 3 2 1

Acquisitions editor: Kelly Reed
Managing editor: Claire Chun
U.S. editor: Anna Dizon
Proofreader: Lauren Harrison
Production: Judith Metzener
Cover design: what!design @ whatweb.com

Distributed by Publishers Group West

The limerick form is complex,
Its contents deal mainly with sex.
It burgeons with virgins
And masculine urgin's,
And a wealth of erotic effects.

—◦◦◦—

A girl who was touring Zambezi
Said, "Attracting men is quite easy:
I don't wear my pants
And, at every chance,
I stand where it's frightfully breezy."

—◦◦◦—

A remarkable fellow named Clarence
Had learned self-control from his parents;
With his wife in the nude
He'd just sit there and brood,
And practice the art of forbearance.

These limericks are callous and crude,
Their morals distressingly lewd;
They're not worth the reading
By persons of breeding—
They're designed for us vulgar and rude.

A pussy just ain't gonna purr,
Unless it has plenty of fur.
With nothing to stroke,
It's merely a joke.
And I won't be laughing, no sir!

A desperate spinster from Clare
Once knelt in the moonlight all bare
And prayed to her God
For a romp on the sod
And a passerby answered her prayer.

A phobic young virgin called Flynn
Shouted before she gave in:
"It isn't the deed,
Or the fear of the seed,
But the big worm that's shedding its skin!"

———

A young Aussie had a sensitive cock,
So in Sydney he kept it in hock,
'Til a trip to "The Alice"
Excited his phallus
And with semen he covered Ayres Rock.

———

A curious mammal's the beaver,
Not the animal—but the "receiver."
It's a great place to hide
A gent's sausage inside,
A grand prize for the overachiever!

A young man by a girl was desired,
To give her the thrills she required;
But he died of old age
Ere his cock could assuage
The volcanic desires it inspired.

Said a certain old mayor I knew,
"I've been struck from the rolls of *Who's Who*,
Just because I was found
Lying prone on the ground
With the nanny (who is twenty-two)."

An unwashed young girl from the Klondike
Has a body worth quite a long hike.
And her face isn't bad,
Yet she's never been had,
'Cause her odor is rather cod-like.

THE WHORE IN THE CAVE

There once was a hermit called Dave,
Who kept a dead whore in a cave.
"It takes lots of pluck,
To have a cold fuck,
But think of the money I save!"

Another old fellow (not Dave),
Found that dead whore in the cave,
He said, "I'll go first,
And if she don't burst,
I'll come to the entrance and wave."

Well the mayor of the town took the floor,
Said, "His actions we simply deplore!
That old hermit named Dave
With the whore in the cave—
We can't tolerate this anymore!"

Yet one more man whose excitable gland
Made him think this adventure was grand,
Thought fucking cold meat
An unusual treat,
'Til a tit came adrift in his hand.

I once met a beautiful Persian,
A shy one who needed coercion,
So I gave her a smile,
And she thought for a while,
Then allowed me to make an insertion.

———

I once had a puppy named Spot,
Who swam daily in our chamber pot,
I must truly admit,
He stank just like shit,
But I did love that puppy a lot.

———

There was a young man from Calcutta,
Who peeped through a hole in a shutter,
But all he could see,
Were his wife's two bare knees,
And the ass of the man who was up her.

There was a young lady from China,
Who mistook for her mouth, her vagina.
Her clitoris was huge,
She covered it with rouge
And lipsticked her labia minor.

———∞∞∞———

There was a young girl they called Kay,
Who fancied a lay in the hay.
She lay on her back,
And opened her crack,
And the farmer said, "You've made my day!"

———∞∞∞———

A prince with a temper outrageous
Had a palace replete with young pages.
They were used for skullduggery
And much royal buggery,
And he castrated some in his rages.

"Austerity now is the fashion,"
Remarked a young lady with passion.
Then she glanced at the bed,
And quietly said,
"But there's one thing that no one can ration."

———✺———

Three fingers and thumb, what a shame!
Only your wife is to blame!
Plastic bottles are better,
They get slippery when wetter,
And will get lost and ne'er seen again!

———✺———

A detective called Ellery Queen
Has olfactory powers so keen,
He can tell at a flash,
Just by sniffing a vag,
Who the previous tenant has been.

A big baseball fan called Miss Glend,
Was the home team's supporter and friend;
But for her a big match,
Never fired up her snatch,
Like a bat with two balls up her end.

—〰—

There was a young maid from Cape Cod,
Who dreamed she was sleeping with God.
'Twas not the Almighty
Who pulled up her nightie,
'Twas Roger the lodger's big rod!

—〰—

There once was a fellow named Latex,
Who invented a way to have safe sex.
Put a bag on your dick,
Any girl you can stick,
But first you must remove the Playtex.

There was an old maid of Duluth,
Who wept when she thought of her youth,
And the glorious chances,
She'd missed at school dances,
And once in a telephone booth.

———

There was a young fellow named Keith,
Who liked to be fondled beneath.
When the whore used her lips,
He wiggled his hips,
But not when the bitch used her teeth!

———

There once was a man named Booker,
Who only liked to fuck hookers.
One day at the loft,
His dick, it fell off,
So now he's only a looker!

There was a young lesbo named Anna,
Who stuffed her friend's cunt with banana,
Which she sucked bit by bit,
From her partner's warm slit,
In the most approved lesbian manner.

———

There was a young man from Nantucket,
Took a pig to a thicket to fuck it.
Said the pig, "No, I'm queer,
Get away from my rear,
Just come to the front and I'll suck it."

———

There once was a man from Pawtucket,
Who stuck his dick in a socket.
His wife was a bitch,
She turned on the switch,
And off went his tool like a rocket!

Gave a solar-powered cock to my hon,
And she said "It's incredibly fun!
But the minutes of waiting
Can be so frustrating,
When a cloud blows in front of the sun."

———

All the she-apes avoided King Kong,
For his prick was horrendously long,
But a carefree giraffe,
Quaffed his yard and a half,
With a gargling outbreak of song.

———

My eminence stood at full-cock,
Until you first lifted your frock.
The sight of those teeth,
Gnashing down underneath,
Has caused me to go into shock!

There once was a fellow named Leland,
Whose balls hung from here to New Zealand.
Both the North and the South
Would fit in his mouth,
Which kept him perpetually kneelin'.

———

There was a fair maiden called Grace,
Who took all she could in her face,
But a well-endowed lad,
Gave her all that he had,
And blew tonsils all over the place.

———

Said an overworked hooker called Randalls,
Of the dozens of men that she handles,
"When I get this busy,
My cunt gets so jizzy,
That it runs down my legs like wax candles."

Yes, Mexico's trees are quite full
Of spuds that all Northern girls pull;
They're shaped like *el toro*,
Just perfect to burrow
In twats, leaving them full of bull.

———∽∾∽———

There once was a man named Harry,
Whose willy was so very scary.
When taking a piss,
It would moan and would hiss,
And was almost too heavy to carry.

———∽∾∽———

There was a young lady called Riddle,
Who had an untouchable middle.
She acquired many friends
Because of her ends,
For it isn't the middle you diddle.

One sailor was thought quite a twit
'cause with girls he just never could hit.
'Til a whore in Hung Chow,
Gave him lessons on "How..." —
Now he gets girls all lickety-split!

———

A well-endowed man from Toledo,
Was cursed with excessive libido.
To buttfuck and screw,
Take fellatio, too,
Were the three major points of his credo.

———

A prudish young maiden called Rose,
Is particular how men propose.
When they say, "Intercourse?"
She replies, "Yes, of course,"
But to "Fuck?" she just turns up her nose.

A horny old miser called Fletcher
Grew tired of being known as a lecher.
In a spasm of meanness,
He cut off his penis,
And now he regrets it, I betcha!

—◦◦◦—

Enjoying a jolly was Molly,
Bent over her food-shopping trolley,
In teeny bikini,
Abusing zucchini,
Bananas and squashes, by golly!

—◦◦◦—

There was an old bishop of Eltham,
Who wouldn't fuck girls, but he felt 'em.
In lanes he would linger
And play stinky finger,
And moan with delight when he smelt 'em.

There once was a gay fellow named Dan,
He was fixing his low-riding van,
When the belt of his garter,
Got caught on the starter,
He screamed and the shit hit the fan!

———

There was a young fellow from Cuba,
Who stuck his dick into a tuba,
Then his newlywed bride
Blew on the other side,
And off flew his dick to Aruba.

———

To his girl said the lynx-eyed detective,
"Is my eyesight the least bit defective?
Has your east tit the least bit
The best of your west tit,
Or is it a trick of perspective?"

Nymphomaniacal Jill,
Tried dynamite for a thrill.
They found her vagina,
Way over in China,
And bits of her tits in Brazil.

———

There once was a lover called Neeky,
Who poked at his babe with his beaky,
She said, "It's no fiction;
I'm fond of the friction,
Compared to your wang it's more squeaky."

———

A liberal lass had a belief,
She could fuck an old man with her teeth.
She complained that he stunk,
Not so much from the spunk,
But his asshole was just underneath.

There was a young pair from Uganda,
Who were fucking out on the veranda.
The juice of their fucks,
Fed forty-two ducks,
Three geese and a furry Great Panda.

A hot-tempered girl of Caracas,
Was wed to a samba-mad jackass.
When he started to cheat her
With a dark señorita,
She kicked him right in the maracas.

There once was a young girl from Hitchen,
Who was scratching her crotch in the kitchen.
Her mother said "Rose,
It's crabs, I suppose?"
Rose said, "Never! Go back to your knittin.'"

There once was a maiden from Arden,
Who sucked off her man in the garden.
He said, "Darling Flo,
Where does my sperm go?"
She replied (swallowing hard), "Beg your pardon?"

⟶⟵

There was a young lady, you see,
Whose hymen was split into three.
And when she was diddled,
The middle string fiddled,
"Nearer, My God, to Thee."

⟶⟵

There once was a whore named Jade,
The most sought-after trick in the trade.
When she died she was laid,
Then relaid in the shade,
And no man will since part with his spade!

There was an old man from Harrow,
Who tried to have sex with a sparrow.
The sparrow said, "No,
You can't have a go,
As the hole in my ass is too narrow."

—∞—

There was a fair lady at sea,
Who said, "How it hurts me to pee."
"I see," said the mate,
"That accounts for the state
Of the captain, the purser and me."

—∞—

There was an old guy from Calcutta,
Who greased up his asshole with butter.
Instead of the roar
Which emitted before,
Came a soft, oleaginous flutter.

Connoisseurs of coitus aver,
That the best British girls never stir.
This condition in Persia,
Is known as inertia:
It depends what response you prefer.

—◦◦◦—

There once was a man from Purdue,
A magician was he, that was true.
Performing a trick,
He vanished his prick,
And now he's become a "sadhu."

—◦◦◦—

'Twas a girl named Laura McTore,
Who was world-renowned as a whore.
Her breasts, they were runts,
But she had fifteen cunts,
She could service a whole team and more.

There once was a priest from Dundee,
Who went in the alley to pee.
"*Dominiscus Nobiscum*,
Oh, why won't the piss come,
It must be the C. L. A. P.!"

———∽∽∽———

Going down on my wife in our bed,
The chandelier fell down on my head.
If she didn't like this,
Darn cunnilingus,
It would have landed on my ass instead.

———∽∽∽———

An indelicate fellow from Ealing,
Was devoid of all sociable feeling.
When a sign on the door
Read, "Don't shit on the floor,"
He jumped up and pooped on the ceiling.

The wife of a chronic crusader
Took on every man who waylaid her;
`Til the amorous itch,
Of this popular bitch,
So annoyed the crusader he spayed her!

———

A young lady got married in Chester,
Her mother—she kissed and she blessed her.
Says she, "You're in luck,
He's a bloody good fuck,
For I had him myself down in Big Sur."

———

An unfortunate lady named Dot,
Had an overabundance of snot.
But it wasn't her nose
That dripped onto her clothes;
From the smell I'd say it was her twat!

There was a young man from Newcastle,
Who received a brown paper parcel.
In it was shit,
And on it was writ,
"A message to you from my asshole."

—⁓—

There was a young writer called Twain,
Whose cock had a sinister stain,
And when he bent down,
You could see it was brown,
And was said to wash off in the rain.

—⁓—

A girl I once knew named Melania,
Used to lick her own boobs with her tongue, yeah!
But she'd suck them too hard,
For one day, on her yard,
They sprayed milk out: Don't get any on ya.

YOUNG BERT

Young Bert was checking out the girlies,
And dropping them all off quite early.
`Til he asked sweet Lydia,
"Please tell me, why did ya
Shave off all of your short and curlies?"

Says she, "Seeing how you've been peeking,
Here's the answer that you are a-seeking:
It won't tickle your nose,
Or your long hose,
When juices I am a-leaking!"

Says he, "I'm peeking and feeling what's leaking,
And down into your panties I'm sneaking,
And when it is bare,
Be sure I'll be there,
With what it is you have been seeking!"

In the Garden of Eden lay Adam,
Complacently stroking his madam,
And great was his mirth,
For on all of this earth,
There were only two balls and he had 'em.

A pervert who lived in Khartoum,
Was exceedingly fond of the womb.
He thought nothing finer
Than a woman's vagina,
And kept three or four in his room.

Today I sat down in Nell's lap,
Between her huge legs was a gap,
Which then opened wide,
And I fell right inside;
I found my way out with a map!

Honestly, it's not water I'm duckin',
While gallons of beer I may suck in.
The source of my fear,
Is perfectly clear,
I don't drink that which fish like to fuck in.

———

There once was a man from Madras,
Who's balls were constructed of brass.
When jangled together,
They played "Stormy Weather,"
And lightening shot out of his ass!

———

We knows three young ladies from Cuxham,
And whenever we meets 'em, we fucks 'em.
When that game grows stale,
We sits on a rail,
We pulls out our pricks, and they sucks 'em.

There was an old man from Corfu,
Who fed upon cunt juice and spew.
When he couldn't get that,
He ate what he shat,
And really good shit he shat, too.

———

A considerate stripper called Jane,
Donned a skirt of thin cellophane.
When asked why she wore it,
She said, "I abhor it,
But my cunt juice would spatter like rain."

———

A student of music from Sparta,
Was widely renowned as a farter.
On the strength of one bean,
She'd fart "God Save the Queen,"
And Beethoven's "Moonlight Sonata."

There once was a man named McQueen,
Who invented a wanking machine.
On the ninety-ninth stroke
The stupid thing broke,
And whipped both his balls up for cream.

There was a young lad from Cosham,
Who took out his balls just to wash 'em.
His mother said, "Jack,
If you don't put 'em back,
I'll jump on 'em both and I'll squash 'em."

There was a young man from Peru,
Whose lineage was noble all through.
It's surely not crud,
Not only his blood,
But even his semen was blue.

Well, Hortense may be like that singer,
Who diddled herself and would linger,
For days at a time,
With feelings sublime,
While sniffing the whiff on her finger.

———

An ancient old whore named McGee,
Was just the right sort for a spree,
Said she, "For a fuck,
I charge half a buck,
And throw in the asshole for free."

———

There once was a man from Kildare,
Whose ass was all covered in hair.
I tried to direct him
To find his lost rectum,
So he shaved it and out fell a chair.

REINCARNATION

In each of my previous lives,
I had numerous girlfriends and wives,
Who in each incarnation,
Bore the next generation,
Into which my dead spirit revives.

But the last time around I did not;
I wasted my time smoking pot,
I forgot to beget,
So I'm not quite here yet,
Someone else is here filling my slot.

So don't bitch if the verse is too weighty,
Someone ELSE wrote the previous eighty,
And now eighty-one:
While I've just begun,
A spirit vacation in Haiti.

An experienced hooker, Arlene,
Said, "Give me a lad of eighteen.
His pecker gets harder,
There's more cream in his larder,
And he fucks with a vigor obscene."

———

I knew a whore from Carolina,
Who had a stupendous vagina.
To save a long line,
She had six at a time,
And another one working behind her.

———

There once was a man made of tin,
With no heart beneath his gray skin.
By a sheer stroke of luck,
He learned how to fuck,
And lived happy in a world full of sin.

An ancient old tart from Silesia,
Said she, "As my cunt doesn't please ya,
You might as well come
Up my slimy old bum,
But beware that my tapeworm don't seize ya."

———

There once was a young girl named Kris,
From Canada who liked to kiss,
But it's girls she adores,
Not men in their drawers,
'Cause they smell and they stand up to piss.

———

A seedy old poet named Dick
Tried to write a good limerick.
His efforts energetic,
Gave results so pathetic,
That hearing it made his friends sick!

A ne'er-do-well slacker from Kent,
Had his wife fuck the landlord for rent,
But as her cunt dried,
The landlord's lust died,
And now they camp out in a tent.

Sir Reggie von Hubble of Joyce
Shaved his balls—it was his choice.
He sneezed, oh how sad!
The results were quite bad!
He now has a very high voice.

There once was a young girl called Dot,
Whose pussy was smokingly hot.
A young lad called Mick,
Once burned off his dick.
Coincidence? Well, maybe not.

A vigorous whore from Warsaw,
Fucked all of her customers raw.
She would thump with her rump,
And punt with her cunt,
And suck every prick that she saw.

———

A frisky young maid named Jeanette,
Married an old baronet.
His prick made her laugh
So, with butler and staff,
She made up a sexy sextet.

———

Thus spoke the old Bey from Algiers,
"I've been whoring around for long years,
And my language is blunt:
A cunt is a cunt,
And fucking is fucking!" (Loud cheers.)

The appeal of a whore in Bengot
Was the absence of hair on her spot.
It was smooth as a dream,
Not through shaving or cream,
But through all of the fucking she got.

———

A few months ago I admit
I could not get enough of Kate's slit.
I would hump every night,
In ecstatic delight,
At her firmness and tightness of fit.

———

There was a young fellow named Bubb,
Who played with himself in the tub.
Massaging his balls,
He shot on the walls,
While farting out rub-a-dub-dub.

MR. JONES AT THE HAREM

Mr. Jones somehow got in a harem,
He had balls, and he chose there to bare 'em.
There arose such a shriek,
He was deaf for a week,
As they fought over how they would share 'em.

He had balls when he came to the harem,
And he thought that no one could impair 'em,
But the ecstatic shriek,
Had alerted the sheik,
Who decided he'd no longer wear 'em.

Now Jones still resides at the harem,
After efforts were made to prepare him,
For his job as a guard ...
Well, it never gets hard,
And there's girls, though he never can snare 'em.

A genetic engineer, Mr. Pickens,
Gave his lab assistant the dickens!
He had saturated a turd,
With the DNA of some bird,
And got some shit that tastes like chicken.

There was a young virgin of Perth,
Swore she'd do it for no one on earth,
Yet she fell without scandal,
To a red Christmas candle,
And was always less choosy henceforth.

There was a young sailor named Fred,
He once took a mermaid to bed.
He said, "To be blunt,
I can't find your cunt,
So why don't you blow me instead?"

A scrofulous woman from Chester,
Said to the man who undressed her,
"I think you will find
That it's better behind,
The front is beginning to fester."

———∿∿∿———

There once was a man from Rangoon,
Who was born two weeks too soon.
He was born by luck,
For it wasn't a fuck,
He was wanked off and tipped in by spoon.

———∿∿∿———

There once was a fellow named Jim,
Who mounted a young girl named Kim.
When he entered her cunt,
He gave a great grunt.
She said, "Oh my, how you've grown, Tim."

The teacher said, "Johnny, be good!"
Said Johnny, "I would if I could,
But the size of your hole,
Makes my willy seem droll,
And it won't stay in place like it should."

A saggy old matron named Dot,
Just sighed as her nipples got hot...
Her tits were adroop,
In her clam chowder soup,
So she tied them both up in a knot.

I once stopped a Turkey named Gobble,
To ask why he walked with a wobble.
"The cook has been pressing,
My ass full of dressing,
And it gives me a bit of a hobble."

There once was a guy named Dave,
Who wanted a good close shave.
His razor did stick,
He cut off his dick,
And now he's a eunuch slave.

———

"My back aches, my penis is sore,
I simply can't fuck anymore.
I'm dripping with sweat,
And you haven't come yet,
And, my God, it's quarter past four!"

———

There once was a girl named Miss Smith,
Who took corn to the mill to make grist with.
The miller's son, Jack,
Laid her flat on her back,
And united the organs they piss with.

THE KNIGHT

"Oh what's all this ailing, armed Knight?
Loitering is plainly not right!
Fuck the sedge and the lake
And that mute bird forsake,
Just tell me about your sad plight."

"I met a neat chick in the Meads...
I set her on one of my steeds...
She made a sweet moan,
Which stiffened my bone,
While I made her a garland of weeds.

"This moaning went on all day long,
While giving me glances sidelong...
Said she'd relish my root,
Add some honey to boot,
And swore that she'd do me no wrong.

"We finally got to her grotto
(By then, on that dew, I was blotto)...
She started to bawl,
I could sense a long haul
Ere my prick and her cunt were legato.

"All those sighs and that kissing, a bore!
I just about left through her door,
But she lulled me to sleep,
That tease of a creep!
I dreamt she enthralled me, that whore!"

So you see here a horny young Knight,
Who sojourns with tale all too trite...
Should have focused on twat,
In that damn elfin grot,
And screwed her with all of his might!

There once was a lady from Glee,
Who was raped by an ape in a tree.
The result was quite horrid,
All ass and no forehead,
Six balls and a purple goatee.

The Postmaster General cried "Asshole!
A pair of bull's balls in a parcel,
Stamped IRA,
With nine pence to pay,
Addressed to the Queen, Windsor Castle!"

A torrid young man from Stamboul,
Had so hot and tumescent a tool,
That each female crater,
Explored by this satyr,
Seemed almost unpleasantly cool.

There were two Greek girls of Miletus,
Who said, "We wear gadgets that treat us,
When strapped on the thigh,
Up cozy and high,
To constant, convenient coitus."

———

There once was a tart called Maggie,
Whose nips were hairy and saggy.
When she opened her bucket,
The blokes wouldn't fuck it,
'Cause both of her lips were so baggy.

———

There was a young man named Paul,
Who had a rectangular ball.
The square of his date,
Plus his penis times eight,
Was two-fifths of five-eights of fuck all.

There was a young fellow called Runyon,
Whose penis developed a bunion.
With every erection,
This painful infection,
Gave off a strong odor of onion.

—⟋⟍⟋⟍—

Young Matilda's twin brother, Matildo,
Made his sister's life wholly fulfilled-o.
He knew it was sin
To stick his dick in,
So instead he just stuck in a dildo.

—⟋⟍⟋⟍—

So, President Bill, that old dreamer,
Sat thinking of women and wieners.
"Isn't it rich,
The dirty young bitch,
Has she never heard of dry cleaners?!"

There once was a Senator from Mass.,
Who was searchin' around for a lass;
He lucked out and found it;
He fucked up and drowned it.
And that was the end of his ass!

—◈—

There was a young novice called Bell,
Who didn't like cunt all that well.
He would finger and fuck one,
But never could suck one.
He couldn't get used to the smell.

—◈—

A squeamish young student named Brand
Adored caressing his gland.
But he viewed with distaste
The gelatinous paste
That it left in the palm of his hand.

TWO YOUNG GIRLS AND THE BISHOP

There once were two young girls from Birmingham,
I knew a wild story concerning 'em.
They lifted the frock,
And diddled the cock,
Of the Bishop engaged in confirming 'em.

Now the Bishop was nobody's fool,
He'd been to a fine public school.
He shifted his britches,
And buttfucked the bitches,
With his twelve-inch Episcopal tool.

But that didn't startle these two,
They laughed as the Bishop withdrew.
The Vicar is quicker
And thicker and slicker
And longer and stronger than you!"

GWEN

I said, as she fucked fast and furious,
"Gwen? Please forgive me, I'm curious.
Dildos that wide
And that long inside,
Are surely to goodness injurious."

"Most certainly not," panted Gwen,
As she fucked herself using a twenty inch dildo and grunt-
ed, "My cavernous cunt
Can accommodate thousands of them."

There was a sweet maiden called Dowd,
Whom a young lecher groped in a crowd.
But the thing that most vexed her
Was when he stood next to her
And said, "I do like your cunt" right out loud.

———

I know of a story that's fraught
With disaster—of balls that got caught,
When a chap took a crap
In the woods, then a trap
Underneath ... Oh, I can't bear the thought.

———

A lady, an expert on skis,
Went out with a man who said, "Please,
On the next precipice,
Will you give me a kiss?"
She said, "Quick, before somebody sees!"

A grumpy and gloomy old Druid,
A pessimist, if he but knew it,
Said, "The world's on the skids
And I think having kids
Is a waste of our seminal fluid."

A scandal involving an oyster,
Sent the Countess of Clewes to a cloister.
She preferred it, in play,
To the Count, they all say,
Being longer, and stronger, and moister.

The old woman who lived in her shoe,
Found a new man she wanted to screw.
She said, "Let us fuck!"
He said, "You must suck!"
Well, this story is strange, but it's true.

A snobbish young woman named Charity,
Finds men who can sate her a rarity,
So she uses a carrot,
Wrapped in fur of a ferret,
Which brings her to bliss with celerity.

———✦———

There once was an old Irish Mick,
Whose cum was exceedingly thick.
He could squeeze it out,
And spray it about,
But it stuck to the end of his dick.

———✦———

There once was a lady from Madras,
Who didn't know what to do with 'er ass.
She wanted to fart,
And tried with all heart,
And now it is just shit that she has.

Even now there's a very great span
'Twixt the viewpoints of woman and man.
Just watch each face change,
When they hear this exchange:
Why's a dog lick his prick? 'Cause he can!

———≈———

There was a young Brit in Madrid,
Who got fifty fucks for a quid.
When they said, "Aren't you faint?"
He replied, "No, I ain't,
But I don't feel as well as I did."

———≈———

There once was guy called Big Bob;
But, strangely, he had a small knob.
So to give his girl pleasure,
Every night beyond measure,
He just used a corn on the cob!

Said a former Prince Regal of Wales:
"I know now what marriage entails,
So I don't want a girl,
But a jolly young earl,
To solace my passion for males."

—∾∾—

Another young maid from New York
Chose to plug up her cunt with a cork.
A woodpecker or two
Made the grade, it is true,
But it utterly baffled the stork.

—∾∾—

There once was a woman from Ealing,
Who had a peculiar feeling.
She lay on her back
And opened her crack,
And pissed all over the ceiling.

FOREPLAY

I'm impressed by the rod that you hold,
Your advances are really quite bold.
But hang on a mo'
'Fore my twat I show,
Warm your hands, they are really too cold!

The warm spot I've found is the best;
Now that you are partly undressed
And both of these mounds
Have warmth that abounds,
Please warm both my hands on your chest.

Caress my chest with your hand,
My God! That feels really grand.
And when you are done,
Don't forget your tongue,
Place it down there on my gland!

Now both of those mounds have a point;
I'll find one more point to anoint.
Around it my tongue
Will bring you unstrung,
And soon you will cry for my joint.

How nice of you to notice my nips,
And place your tongue on the very tips.
Now don't be afraid,
If you want to get laid,
Place your head 'tween my legs and take sips.

Culture and pussy? Oh please!
I once had a girl on her knees;
When our humping updrafted,
The aroma that wafted,
Sure smelled like a well-cultured cheese.

———

A lady who thought sex a treat
Thought a gang-bang would make life complete.
Fifteen men and a dog
All went the whole hog,
And she staggered back home down the street.

———

There once was a whore from Peru,
Who filled her pussy with glue.
She said with a grin,
"You pay to get in,
And you pay to get out of it, too."

As Tarzan swung home through the air,
Natives saw that his ass was quite bare.
He went home to wife Jane,
His noble face filled with pain,
To admit he lost her underwear.

———

A wandering Munchkin named Syfe,
Heard a most terrible strife.
The loud grinding and shearing,
Led him to a clearing,
Where the Tin Man was fucking his wife.

———

There was a young lady of Wells
Whose cervix was festooned with bells.
Whenever she'd come,
Her vagina would hum,
Just like the "Bolero"—Ravel's.

There was an old tart from Marseilles,
Washed her cunt with a high-pressure spray.
She said, "Ah that's better,
I've found a French letter,
That's been missing since last Christmas Day."

—∿—

There once was a redneck called Jim,
Who liked his girls fat more than slim.
"If she's bigger, she's better;
If she's tubby, I'll get her;
Because big girls have very fine quim."

—∿—

Said the Duchess of Chester at tea,
"Young man, do you fart when you pee?"
I replied with some wit,
"Do you belch when you shit?"
I think that was one up to me!

There once was a woman from Clyde,
Who fell into an outhouse and died.
The next day her brother,
Fell into the other,
And now they're in turd side-by-side.

———

There was a young gaucho called Bruno,
Who said, "There's one thing that I do know.
A woman is fine,
A boy is divine,
But a llama is *numero uno*."

———

A whiff of her natural scent,
Will stimulate many a gent.
But waiting a month
Before washing her cunt,
Is only for those the most bent.

A willing Scots lass called McFargle,
Without coaxing and such argle-bargle,
Would suck a man's pud
Just as hard as she could,
And save up the sperm for a gargle.

There once was a girl from Nantucket
Who rode to hell in a bucket,
But when she got there
They asked for her fare,
So she pulled up her skirt and said, "Fuck it."

An excitable lady called Donna,
Got wed to an expert embalmer.
He filled up her cracks
With resin and wax,
Attempting to soothe and to calm her.

'Twas sad when we finally parted,
And tears pricked my eyes as I started
To sob, 'til she said,
"Love, I'll miss you in bed
For you kept me quite warm when you farted."

———∽∽∽———

There once was a man from Uppingham,
Who stood on the bridge at Buckingham,
Just watching the stunts
Of the cunts in the punts,
And the tricks of the pricks that were fucking them.

———∽∽∽———

A randy young man from the Cape
Was trying to rape an ape.
The ape said, "You fool,
You'll damage your tool,
And you're putting my ass out of shape."

CHUCK GOES TO THE GYM

Though Chuck is a tiny bit dim,
He's quite healthy in body and limb,
But he's running to fat.
"I must see about that,"
He said, "Think I'll go down to the gym."

Receptionist, dopey Louise
(With a bandage or two round her knees)
Said to Chuck, "Let me see;
It's a five dollar fee,"
And "Atchoo!" she started to sneeze.

"She's healthy," thought Chuck with a grin
As he walked through the door labeled "IN,"
And inside took a peek
At the bodies so sleek
And the ladies remarkably thin.

He went through the changing room door;
Dropped his jeans and his shirt to the floor;
Took off his shoes and socks
And then removed his jocks
And hung them on peg number 4.

"Oh bother!" he thought, "Holy shit!
In reception I've left all my kit."
And forgetting his state
Of undress he went straight
Back the way he came in. (Silly twit.)

(Of course he got lost.) He went sneaking
Quite naked through corridors peeking
Round doors for a sight
Of reception and fright-
ened the ladies who ran away shrieking.

A cop with a bulletproof vest
Shouted, "Pervert, you're under arrest
For the mayhem you've caused."
Then he looked at him, paused,
And said, "Chuck! You're a damn awful pest."

Have you heard the sad tale of young Lockett?
He was blown off his feet by a rocket.
The force of the blast
Blew his balls up his ass,
And his penis was found in his pocket.

———

A dignified lady of York,
Tried to eat crap on a fork.
Her son cried, "You goon,
You eat shit with a spoon,
It's pork that you eat with a fork!"

———

I once met an alien from Venus,
Who had an incredible penis.
When I touched it, it glowed
And began to explode,
All over and all in between us.

Her frustration was so hard to handle
And she thought diddling no real scandal.
But her fingers went numb
And she still hadn't come,
So she opted to try out a candle.

———

There once was a lady from Sydney,
Who could take it right up to the kidney.
Then a man from Quebec
Took it up to her neck.
He had a big one, now, didn't he?

———

There once was a whore in the school,
Who thought that it would be too cool,
To go out and get it;
Screw teachers for credit.
What a fucked-up and slovenly fool!

Oh, Lord! How the air did turn green
When a fart came straight out of the queen!
The court sat aghast
At the loud royal blast,
So they stood and sang "God Save the Queen."

—◦◦◦—

There once was a girl from Vancouver,
Who had an affair with her Hoover.
With a passionate twitch,
She kicked on the switch,
And it took several men to remove her.

—◦◦◦—

A lascivious fellow called Lees,
Loved to give his poor cock a long squeeze.
This continual friction
Made real sex a mere fiction,
But the callus hung down to his knees.

A girl with magnificent tits,
When dancing would wiggle her hips;
A wonderful flirt,
She'd lift up her skirt,
And exhibit her sensuous lips.

———

There once was a cat that purred,
"I want milk instead of curd!"
He went walking at noon
And was chased by a coon
Into a pile of dog turd!

———

There once was a man named Mort,
Whose dick was decidedly short.
When he climbed into bed,
His lady friend said,
"That's not a dick, it's a wart."

I'm not sure if this is a cum hole;
It might be the young lady's bung hole.
But I'll take a chance—
And put in my lance—
Hey, hey, hey, it sure is a fun hole!

———

I recall an old man from Duluth,
Whose cock was shot off in his youth.
He fucked with his nose,
And his fingers and toes,
And he came through a hole in his tooth.

———

There once was a man from Cape Fear,
Who had a big dick for an ear.
He said, "Sex could last long,
If your neck is real strong,
And you don't catch your ear in your rear."

The good wife of a sportsman called Chuck,
Found her married life clean out of luck.
Her husband played hockey,
Not wearing a jockey,
Now he ain't got what it takes for a fuck.

—◦◦◦—

There was a young girl from the Cape,
Filled her hole with bicycle tape,
To ease the pangs,
Caused by the bangs,
Of gentlemen bent upon rape.

—◦◦◦—

When his friend's turn came to pass,
He took in a bundle of grass,
To make a soft buffer,
To protect, when he stuffed her,
His prick if it poked through her ass.

There once was a man from South Bend,
Whose wife caught him fucking her friend.
He said, "It's no use, Duck,
Interrupting this fuck,
For I'm damned if I draw 'til I spend."

Arabella's a terrible prude;
She says, "Men are beasts. Men are lewd.
A girl has to watch
Or their hand's in her crotch,
And the next thing she knows, she is screwed."

I'll warn you here, lads, about Jane,
An expert in smuggling cocaine.
Don't give her a shag,
For that ten-kilo bag
Of crack in her crack will cause pain.

An eager young fellow from Norway,
Tried to jerk himself off in a sleigh.
But the air was so frigid,
It froze his balls rigid,
And all he produced was frappé.

A cardinal living in Rome,
Had a Renaissance bath in his home.
He would savor the nudes,
As he worked up his moods,
In emulsions of semen and foam.

There once was a man from Bombay,
Who fashioned a cunt out of clay.
But the heat from his prick,
Turned the damn thing to brick,
And it ripped all his foreskin away.

There was a young girl of Baroda,
Who built an erotic pagoda;
The walls of its halls
Were festooned with the balls
And the tools of the fools that bestrode her.

⟋⟋⟍

I was so enamored with Randall,
That I let him insert a candle,
But then came the match
Which burned up my snatch.
I guess now I'm too hot to handle!

⟋⟋⟍

Thomas Turkey was a handsome slugger,
His wife was sure fond of his sugar.
But on Thanksgiving morn,
He was stuffed full of corn,
By the cook, who was a real bugger.

When Angelico worked in cerise,
For an angel, he painted his niece.
In a heavenly trance
He whipped off her pants,
And erected a fine altarpiece.

———

There was an old lecher from Critch,
Had the syph and the clap and the itch.
His name was McNabs
And he also had crabs,
That dirty old son-of-a-bitch.

———

A funky but cute fortuneteller,
Was dating a weird sort of feller.
On a doctor's advice
She was treated for lice,
But really, you don't want to smell 'er.

A naughty old lady of Spain,
Decided she'd have to abstain.
But plugging the entry,
That favored the gentry,
Excited the lady again.

———

THE MAN FROM DEVIZES

There was a young man from Devizes
Whose balls were of different sizes.
The left one was small,
Almost no ball at all,
And the right one was large and won prizes.

We revisit the man from Devizes
With testicles of different sizes.
We women don't care
If his balls are a pair—
It's the bit in the middle we prizes!

There once was a man from Bulgaria,
Who went for a piss in an area.
Said waiter to cook,
"Oh, do come and look,
Have you ever seen anything hairier?"

There was a young lady from Bude,
Who went on the stage in the nude.
One night out in front,
A man shouted, "Cunt!"
Out loud, just like that, fucking rude!

A lady of features cherubic
Was famed for her area pubic;
When they asked its size,
She said with surprise,
"Are you speaking of square feet, or cubic?"

Ophelia, feeling no pain,
And freed from the need to abstain,
Declared it was better
With big Irish setters.
(She'd been fucked quite enough by Great Danes.)

There was a young fellow from Harrow,
Who had one very big marrow.
He said to his tart,
"Try this for a start.
My balls are outside on a barrow."

A prisoner of Chateau d'If,
Ran around on all fours for a sniff
Of his comrade's posterior,
And said, "It's inferior,
But it somehow reminds me of quiff."

A lesbian lady called Maud,
Did well in the Army by fraud.
Her tongue, quite infernal,
Slipped into the colonel,
And now she's a major, by God!

—ᴍᴍ—

There was a young whore from Kilkenny,
Who charged two fucks for a penny.
For half of that sum,
You could bugger her bum,
An economy practiced by many.

—ᴍᴍ—

Leo and Scott played tennis,
In a quiet little town near Venice.
They used special balls,
That used to be Paul's,
And now Paul feels quite tremendous.

A bear taking a dump asked a rabbit,
"Does shit stick to your fur as a habit?"
"Of course not," said the hare,
"It's really very rare!"
So the bear wiped his ass with the rabbit.

⎯⎯⎯

She squatted while diddling her clit,
Embedding it deep in her slit.
But she got so excited,
The candle ignited,
And singed her caboodle and kit.

⎯⎯⎯

A tongue-tied man from Fort Worth,
Had a dick with tremendous girth.
He said with a grin,
As he slid it on in,
"I can thee that I am not your firth."

An unusual nurse from Japan
Lifted men by their pricks to the pan.
A trick of jujitsu,
And, either it shits you,
Or makes you feel more of a man.

—

There was a young lady called Hilda,
Who went for a walk with a builder.
She knew that he could,
That he should, and he would,
And he did, and it damn near killed her.

—

An enormously fat girl, Miss Dinah,
Employed a young water diviner,
To play a slick trick,
With his prick as a stick,
To help her locate her vagina.

AT THE BOUTIQUE

A gent at a sexy boutique,
Eyed the sales girl, Dominique.
He said, "I'm just sniffin',
Your stuff is quite spiffin'
But a musk scent is more what I seek."

She said, "I'll just check in the back..."
And returned with some panties in black.
He sniffed with delight,
The scent was just right!
She smiled and said, "Twat has that knack!"

———

There was a young lad from the Falls,
Who used to perform in the halls.
His favorite trick
Was to stand on his prick
And roll off the stage on his balls.

There once was a Queen of Bulgaria,
Whose bush had grown hairy and hairier,
'Til a Prince from Peru,
Who came up for a screw,
Had to hunt for her cunt with a terrier.

—✺—

There was a young whore from Tashkent,
Who commanded an immoral rent.
Day out and day in
She lay writhing in sin,
Giving thanks it was ten months to Lent.

—✺—

He's climbing Mount Baldy again.
This jerk's such a pervert, 'cause when
He has these gals shave,
He thinks he's so brave,
Pretending they're children of ten.

I've a trick that could earn money soon,
For by angling my lips with a spoon,
And arching my back,
To lengthen my crack,
I can get it to whistle a tune.

———

There was a young couple from Florida,
Whose passion grew steadily torrider;
They had planned to sin
At a room in the inn,
But, impatient, they screwed in the corridor.

———

A Paris-based artist named Sayer
As a cubist was really quite fair.
He searched all his life
To find him a wife,
Possessed of a cunt that was square.

There once was a man from South Ealing,
Who found his prick highly appealing,
But not to feel dumb,
He made his hand numb.
It was like someone else he was feeling.

—∞—

There was a young woman, a Brit,
Who had a both a short and long tit.
But what made her a catch
Was her lopsided snatch
And the tricks she could do with it.

—∞—

There once was a man from Seattle,
Whose dick was cut off in a battle.
He said, "Holy Shit!
It looks like a clit."
And now he whacks off with a paddle.

"Is this girl the same one who trains parrots?
Or, perhaps, she's the one who digs ferrets?
If she's one and the same,
Will you give me her name?
Blows my mind what this girl does with carrots."

There once was a man from down under,
When he fucked it sounded like thunder.
He said, "Hey there, mate!
Why masturbate?
Oh! Look at your dick, it's no wonder."

There once was a girl who liked tarts,
She also made really big farts.
While playing one day,
Off came Dad's toupee,
From the wind of her really big fart.

Love, get off that mechanical steed,
I will give you the ride that you need.
This here saddle horn's hot,
Climb aboard; treat your slot,
And I'll rock you at variable speed!

―――

There was a young man of Australia,
Who painted his ass like a dahlia.
The drawing was fine,
The color divine,
But the scent—alas—was a failure.

―――

A flatulent actor named Barton
Led a life exceedingly spartan.
'Til a playwright one day,
Wrote a well-received play,
With a part in for Barton to fart in.

For widower, wanted: Housekeeper,
Not too refined, but a light sleeper,
When employer's inclined,
Must be game for a grind,
Pay is generous, mind, but can't keep her.

———∿∿∿———

A greengrocer's girl from down under,
The boys thought a really hot number.
When business was slow,
She'd put on a show,
Performing the cucumber rumba.

———∿∿∿———

An elegant fellow, young Saul;
He was able to bounce either ball.
He could stretch 'em and snap 'em,
And juggle and clap 'em,
Which earned him the plaudits of all.

ON THE ENTERPRISE

A girl of the *Enterprise* crew,
Refused every offer to screw,
'Til a Vulcan named Spock,
Crawled under her smock,
And now she is eating for two.

The *Enterprise* girls, so one hears,
Have chased Spock for several years.
His look of disdain,
Has spared them great pain,
For his cock is as sharp as his ears.

The prick of the engineer, Scott,
Fell off from Saturnian Rot,
So he went to the basement,
And made a replacement,
Of tungsten and plastic and snot.

There was once a sailor from Wales,
An expert at pissing in gales.
He could piss in a jar,
From the top gallant spar,
Without even wetting the sails.

—◦◦◦—

There was a young widow from Kent,
With a cunt of enormous extent,
And so deep and so wide,
The acoustics inside
Formed an echo wherever she went.

—◦◦◦—

There was a young lawyer quite bright,
Couldn't fuck 'cause her twat was too tight.
She discovered a loophole,
By using her poophole,
Now she fucks all day and all night.

There once was a fellow named Vic,
Who pleasured himself with a stick.
He once got it stuck
And said, "What the fuck?"
Now there's no room for a prick.

———

There was a young girl of Angina,
Who stretched string across her vagina.
From the lovemaking dock,
With the proper-sized cock,
Came toccata and fugue in D minor.

———

A sex maniac, Mr. Rub-a-dub,
Belonged to the Suck, Fuck, and Bugger Club,
But the joy of his life,
Were the tits of his wife;
One real, and one Indian-rubber dub.

Said a guy to his girlfriend, "Virginia,
For ages I've courted to win ya.
Now my point of frustration,
Has reached saturation—
This evening I gotta get in ya!"

———

Heather, that nasty young troll,
Had an especially humongous hole.
Her twat was so wide,
That in it I'd slide,
Four fingers, a thumb, and a pole.

———

A lady who hailed from Wadesmill,
Sat down on a nearby mole's hill.
The resident mole
Stuck his head up her hole—
The lady's okay, but the mole's ill!

A glutted debauchee from Frome,
Lured beauteous boys to his room,
Whereupon he would strip them,
And generally whip them,
With rods of fine birch or of broom.

—ᴕᴥᴕ—

There was a notorious seaman,
Who with ladies was quite a young demon.
In peace or in war,
At sea or on shore,
He was liberal and free with his semen.

—ᴕᴥᴕ—

The lord of the manor, Sir Stoat,
Suffered from terminal bloat.
He exploded one day,
They found balls in the hay,
And part of his scrote in the moat.

FORGIVENESS

"Forgive me my sins," muttered Father
O'Reilly, "But God I'd much rather
Not have to take mass,
'Til I've seen to this lass
And I've worked up a sweat and a lather."

"Forgiveness? Forgiveness for this!?"
Thundered God, "Are you taking the piss?
Well, okay, if you must,
But hold fire with your lust,
'Til I've had my own way with that miss."

—◦◦◦—

There once was a lady named Cager,
Who, as the result of a wager,
Consented to fart
The entire oboe part
Of Mozart's "Quartet in F Major."

My organ is quite long and fat.
It's played often and never gone flat.
There's adequate measure
For temples of pleasure,
But not in a cathedral like that.

—∿—

There once was a man from Bombay,
Who ate tons of beans ev'ry day.
He farted so loud,
It attracted a crowd,
But the smell made them all run away.

—∿—

There was a sweet lady who said,
As her new beau climbed into her bed,
"I'm tired of this stunt
That they do with one's cunt,
You can slip up my bottom instead."

A posh girl named Tabitha Vickers,
Wore her fur coat without any knickers.
Her soft furry mink
Caused young men to wink,
And ask if she'd like them to lick hers.

———∞———

There once was a fellow named Bob,
Who wanted an ass for his knob,
He bought an old whore,
Went through the back door,
Now he wishes she'd wiped it, the slob!

———∞———

None could better our sex limousine,
With its neat built-in fucking machine:
Engineered, it connects,
To suit either sex,
And adjusts to the fat and the lean.

While fucking his wife, Dr. Zuck
In his ears got his wife's nipples stuck.
With his thumb up her bum,
He could hear himself come,
Thus inventing the "telephone fuck."

—❧—

"I don't like the look of your thatch,
Although I could do with a scratch;
But damn it, my pants
Are advancing. A chance
I shall just have to take with your snatch."

—❧—

A turd dropped by Sister Ecclesia,
Reached from Key West to Southern Rhodesia.
The cause of this dump,
Was a three-foot lump,
Of Ex-Lax with Milk of Magnesia.

There once was a woman named Carrie,
She wished for a guy she could marry.
Her daughter got some,
And she could get none,
So she made do with billy goat Larry.

⎯⎯⎯∞⎯⎯⎯

There was a young girl of Salina,
Who had such a tiny vagina,
Men entered and left,
That diminutive cleft,
And now they have had to reline her.

⎯⎯⎯∞⎯⎯⎯

There was a young stud from Glenchasm,
Who had a stupendous orgasm.
In the midst of his thrall,
He burst both his balls,
And covered an acre with plasm.

There was a young woman from Leeds,
Who swallowed a packet of seeds.
In less than an hour,
Her tits were all flowers,
And her ass—it was covered in weeds.

There was a young man from Capri,
Who tried to piss over a tree.
The tree was too high,
And it fell in his eye,
And now the poor idiot can't see.

There was a young tart from Madrid,
Who was longing to have her a kid.
Then came an Italian,
Hung like a stallion,
Who rode her like Billy the Kid.

Young men pursued Jane with such haste,
That she filled her vagina with paste.
Her reasoning ran:
"I'll hold onto a man,
Or else I'd be better off chaste."

There was a young pansy named Gene,
Who cruised a sadistic Marine.
Said the man with a smirk,
As they got down to work,
"In this game, the Jack beats the Queen."

An innocent maid from Penzance
Decided to take just one chance.
So she let herself go
In the lap of her beau,
And now all her sisters are aunts.

There was a young girl from Eskdale,
Who put her ass up for sale.
For the sum of two bits,
You could tickle her tits,
But a dollar would get you some tail.

———

In her travels, a lady named Dinah
Kept white mice inside her vagina.
When asked for her reason,
She quipped, "They're in season,
And men like to eat them in China."

———

There was a young lady from Dee,
Who slept with each man she did see.
Should it come to a test,
She wished to be best,
And "Practice makes perfect," said she.

BROTHER FRANCIS

Attempting to stop his wet dreams,
Brother Francis has tried many schemes.
Using bells and a whistle,
Attached to his gristle,
But still finds he frequently creams.

So grimly the Abbot said, "Look,
Orgasm's a sin in my book,
Inadvertent or not.
Tie your dick in a knot,
Or start sleeping with Annie the cook.

There was an old fellow from Ealing
His dick with his hand he was feeling
He shot it so high,
Up into the sky,
He looked up as it dripped from the ceiling.

An inquisitive chap from Lapland,
Was informed that fucking was grand.
But at his first trial,
He said with a smile,
"I've had the same feeling by hand."

———

There once was a milkman named Schwartz,
Whose cock was all covered with warts.
But women would play,
With his dick anyway,
Filling their cunts up with quarts.

———

The lady next door has invented,
Some perfumes outrageously scented,
With essence of honey,
And dripping wet cunny;
It drives all the fellows demented.

There was a young man of Belgrade,
Who planned to seduce a fair maid.
And as it befell,
He succeeded quite well,
So the maid, like the plan, was deep-laid.

—⌇—

An unhappy young bride named McBryce,
Had a husband who came in a trice.
But she managed to cool,
His impetuous tool,
By stuffing her cunt with dry ice.

—⌇—

There is a girl from Nantucket,
Whose favorite trick is to suck it.
She likes a big dick,
One she can lick,
She swallows, gets sick, and upchucks it.

THE PREACHER'S DAUGHTER

There once was a preacher's daughter,
Who resented the pony he bought her,
'Til she found that it's dong,
Was as hard and as long,
As the prayers her father had taught her.

Wait, there's more—

She married a chappie named Tony,
Who soon caught her fucking the pony.
He cried, "What's it got,
My dear, that I've not?"
And she sighed, "Just a yard-long baloney."

A well-endowed fellow called Danny,
The size of whose prick was uncanny,
Made his wife, the poor dear,
Take it into her ear,
And it came out the hole in her fanny.

There was an experienced whore,
Who knew all the old coital lore.
She said, "Though it pains us,
Men opt for my anus,
So now I don't fuck any more."

There was a fat turkey named Sam,
Who gobbled whenever he ran.
He came out of the bush,
Presenting his tush,
And was shot up the ass by a man.

As John entered Jane's muff for a dive,
He said, "It's on her pussy I thrive.
Her bush is real boss,
I use it to floss,
And her cunt's like Chanel No. 5."

There once was a girl named Louise,
Whose cunt hair hung down past her knees,
The fleas on her box,
Tied her hair up in knots,
And now it's a flying trapeze.

———

There once was a man from Nantucket,
Who's dick was so long he could suck it.
He said with a grin,
While wiping his chin,
"If my ear were a cunt I could fuck it".

———

A lusty young ranger from Maine,
With no woman for years had he lain.
He found sublimation,
At a high elevation,
In the crotch of a pine—God, the pain!

There was a young girl from Edina,
Shoved avians up her vagina,
As much as she pleased,
'Til one day, she sneezed—
Out popped three swans and a mynah!

———

There was a young lady of Eton,
Whose figure had plenty of meat on.
She said, "Marry me, dear,
And you'll find that my rear
Is a nice place to warm your cold feet on."

———

There once was a fellow named Abbott,
Who made love to girls as a habit;
But he ran for the door,
When one girl asked for more,
And exclaimed, "I'm a man, not a rabbit."

An indolent fellow called Blood,
Made his fortune by being a stud,
With a fifteen-inch thing,
And two balls that would ring,
And a load like the biblical flood.

———

Way down in the depths of Louisa's
Sweet pussy live three tiny geezers;
Rewarding their teasing,
Exceedingly pleasing,
She gives them wee hand-jobs with tweezers.

———

There was a young girl from Detroit,
Who at screwing was very adroit.
She could squeeze her vagina,
To a pin-point, or finer,
Or open it out like a kite.

I'm a mean, nasty, bad-talkin' bastard.
It's a lifestyle I've thoroughly mastered.
But I have to confess,
That the ol' IRS,
Has me beat even when I am plastered.

———

A long time ago I shaved mine,
And I thought it looked perfectly fine—
Virginal and pure,
I felt so demure,
But when they grew back—porcupine!

———

A cautious young lady named Hall,
Has a diamond as big as a ball.
If we told where she keeps
It at night when she sleeps,
Man, you wouldn't believe us at all.

Young Chris to a pretty young miss:
"Bet you ain't got a thingy like this."
"No I ain't, I admits,
But with this (and my tits),
I'll get thousands of those, little Chris."

There was an old fellow called Pewter,
Who often rode out on a scooter.
His favorite trick,
Was to stand on his prick,
And use his bare ass as a hooter.

An overweight lady named Tammy,
Fell over a band in Miami.
All of the brass,
Went up her fat ass,
She farted, and then won a Grammy.

Complaining the measures were meager,
Young Igor, on visiting Riga,
Said, "Vodka in Omsk,
Vladivostok, and Tomsk,
Comes in measures a fucking lot bigger."

———ᕗᕦᕤ———

Liz shrieked and then beat her bare breast;
She said, "Hump me, I'm truly impressed!"
With his dick in her dock,
He caused her to rock,
And singing came out of her nest!

———ᕗᕦᕤ———

There once was a wonderful wizard,
Who had a great pain in his gizzard.
He ate wind and snow,
At fifty below,
And farted a forty-day blizzard.

To your ear, if you hold up a shell,
The ocean you'll hear (so they tell).
But you'll find that you've got
A lot more with twat—Not only the sound, but the smell!

———— ◦⦿◦ ————

An Arab called Abou ben Adhem,
Thus cautioned a traveling madam,
"I suffer from crabs
As do most Arabs."
"It's all right," said madam, "I've had 'em."

———— ◦⦿◦ ————

The man in the bar was real shrewd,
Some may say a little bit lewd.
He reached out his mitts,
To grope for some tits,
But discovered the chest of a dude.

An angler in medieval Nice,
Was instantly ordered to cease,
His naughty deception,
When, during inspection,
They found a real cod in his piece.

———

There once was a man named Bill Odom,
Whose balls were too big for his scrotum.
Though relief he sought,
It all went for naught,
'Cause he didn't know how to unload 'em.

———

When a girl asked the size of his dick,
The Texan responded, right quick,
"Three inches, or four."
"My boyfriend has more!"
"Yes, ma'am. You mean lengthwise, or thick?"

The cock of a fellow called Gable,
Was pliant and long as a cable.
Each eve as he ate,
This suave reprobate
Would screw his wife under the table.

———∿∿∿———

I once went to the Midwest,
'Cause I heard Iowans were the best.
Their plump, juicy, sweet
Cornstalks can't be beat.
Their buttered cobs pumped me with zest!

———∿∿∿———

An insatiable satyr named Frazer,
Is known as a wild woman-chaser.
He's the cause of myriads
Of overdue periods,
For to him "rubber" means an eraser.

An indelicate lady called Bruce,
She captured her man with a ruse:
She packed up her fuselage
With a good, viscous mucilage,
And he never could pry himself loose.

———

Three elderly spinsters of Kent,
Gave up copulation for Lent.
Including door handles,
Both tapers and candles,
And anything else that was bent.

———

There was a lascivious wench,
Whom nothing could ever make flinch.
She'd insert a man's pole,
In just any old hole,
She'd suck it, fuck, jerk-off, and French.

An impoverished fellow from Yale,
Had a face that was notably pale.
He spent his vacation,
In self-masturbation,
Because of the high cost of tail.

———

There was a young lady, Miss Chow,
Who said that she didn't know how.
'Til a young Frenchman caught her,
And jolly well taught her,
And she's living in France with him now.

———

Twenty-thousand leagues under the sea,
Seems pretty deep, if you ask me.
My girlfriend's peeper
Is twelve leagues deeper,
And in it, you scuba for free!

That wicked old Sappho from Greece,
Said, "What makes me feel really at peace,
Is to have my pudenda,
Rubbed hard by the end-o
The little pink nose of my niece."

———∽∾∽———

There once was a man named McViner,
Who searched for the perfect vagina.
Everyday he would hunt,
For this flawless cunt:
I'm flattered, because it was mine-a.

———∽∾∽———

There was a young virgin from Bude,
Whose proclivities were often viewed,
With distrust by the males,
For she'd fondle their tails,
But never would let them intrude.

There lived a young thing in Marseilles,
Who giggled when on the bidet.
It tickled her end,
'Cause her young plumber friend,
Had charged up the pipes with Perrier.

—ᴑᴑᴑ—

There was a young man from Pitlochry,
Making love to his girl in the rock'ry.
She said, "Look you've come
All over my bum.
This isn't a fuck, it's a mock'ry!"

—ᴑᴑᴑ—

A red-headed stripper called Sally,
Regularly performed at the palais.
She got such applause,
When she dropped her drawers,
'Cause the hair on her head did not tally.

There once was a woman of Britain,
Whose pussy was soft as a kitten.
When winter came round,
She quite quickly found
That her twat made a lovely warm mitten.

———

The King gave a lesson in class,
When he was once fondling a lass.
When she used the word "damn,"
He chided, "Please ma'am,
Keep a more civil tongue in my ass."

———

Sailor Uranus is a bit queer,
Her friend Sailor Neptune has no fear,
Because they are lovers,
Playing under the covers,
All you hear is a groan or a cheer.

There was a young fellow named Andy,
And all the girls knew he was randy.
Girls looking like Venus,
Played with his big penis.
One girl said, "That's terribly handy!"

The wife of a warrior Celt
Lost the key to her chastity belt.
She tried picking the lock
With an Ulsterman's cock,
And the next thing he knew, he was gelt.

The pussy's not much of a sight;
To reveal it is thought impolite.
But the pussy appeals
In the way that it feels,
When you slide into mine in the night!

There once was a maitre d'hotel,
Who said, "They can all go to hell!
They make love to my wife,
And it ruins my life,
For the worst is, they do it so well!"

—◦◦◦—

Midsummer Night's Dream's like a fever,
When good old Bottom the Weaver,
Slips his huge member out,
And up the Queen's spout
Without her knowing—who would believe her?

—◦◦◦—

In anything written by Dickens,
It's certain the plot always thickens—
With characters, themes
And digressions it teems;
As for sex, though, it's mighty slim pickin's.

In the war, with their men in the army,
The women were all going barmy.
Alas, that was that,
They could not feed their twat,
Until someone imported salami!

———

There was a young lady from Uttoxeter,
The boys, they all waved their cocks at her.
She contracted the pox,
From one of the cocks.
Now she's poxed all the cocks in Uttoxeter.

———

Said a weary young fellow called Shea,
When his prick wouldn't stand for a lay,
"You must seize it and squeeze it
And tease it and please it,
For Rome wasn't built in a day."

The Right Reverend Dean of St. Just
Was consumed with erotical lust.
He buttfucked three men,
Two mice and a hen,
And a little green lizard that bust.

A maiden who dwelled in Palm Springs,
Had her maidenhead torn into strings
By a hideous Kurd,
And although it's absurd,
When the wind now blows through it, it sings.

A certain young lady named Alice,
Lunched with the King at the palace,
The dirty old King
Said, "Look at my thing!"
And promptly showed her his phallus.

There is a young lady of Ryde,
Whose pussy is massively wide.
You should see the huge numbers
Of squash and cucumbers
And tree trunks she slides up inside.

—

An innocent bride from the mission,
Remarked, on her first night's coition:
"What an intimate section
To use for connection—
And, Lord! What a silly position!"

—

My pussy teeth now are gnashing!
(That gold one in front is flashing!)
I'd probably make you
Into testicle stew,
But I'm squeamish about all the bashing!

There was an old geezer named Crockett,
Who stuck his dick into a socket.
"I hope I don't burn it,
Or otherwise turn it
'Cause I'd miss it if I couldn't cock it."

There was a young harlot from Clyde,
Whose doctor cut open her hide.
He misplaced her stitches,
And closed all her niches,
She now does her work on the side.

There once was an escort named Guy,
Whose company ladies would buy.
They found that his trick,
Was not a big dick,
But a sausage he taped to his thigh.

A lady who "hooks" for a living,
Had no chest, so her profits were thinning.
She got her boobs stuffed,
Now they're quite big enough,
To give a new lift to "Thanksgiving."

───❦───

An innovative fellow called Hunt,
Trained his prick to perform a neat stunt:
This versatile spout,
Could be turned inside out
Like a glove, and be used as a cunt.

───❦───

I did feel obliged to friend Fife,
For the overnight use of his wife.
But he dropped in today,
And insisted on pay—
Such sordidness sours me on life.

A maiden who lived in Virginny,
Had a cunt that could neigh, bark, and whinny.
The hunting set rushed her,
Fucked, buggered, and crushed her,
When the pitch of her organ went tinny.

———

A horrid small girl in Madrid,
A most insensitive kid,
Told her Auntie Louise
That her cunt smelled of cheese,
And the worst of it was that it did!

———

An incorrigible clown from St. James,
Indulged in the jolliest games;
He lighted a match
To his grandmother's snatch,
And laughed as she pissed through the flames.

An arrogant wench from Salt Lake,
Liked to tease all the boys on the make.
She was finally the prize
Of a man twice her size,
And she still remembers the ache.

My horny old aunt, Antoinette,
Inspected me through her lorgnette:
"Your prick's unsurpassed!
I must take a cast!
It'll make such a fine statuette."

There once was a man, name of Jack.
He kept his dick stuck up his crack.
When he sat down,
He went to town,
On his li'l friend he called Zack.

There was a young lady called Moore,
Who, while not quite precisely a whore,
Could not miss the chance
To whip off her pants
To compare a man's stroke with her bore.

—⟳—

I think my teacher is smart,
He has such a wonderful heart;
He said with a grin,
As it rumbled within,
That smell in the air is a fart.

—⟳—

There once was a nude girl named Dinah,
Conceived, born, and raised in China.
When she smiled you'd find
She had four of a kind:
Two each on her face and vagina.

"I'll admit," said a lady called Barr,
"That a penis is like a cigar;
But, in general, to people
A phallic church steeple
Is stretching the subject too far."

———

A self-centered woman named Perkins,
Would work off her urges with gherkins,
Until with a skid,
Inside her one slid,
And pickled her internal workin's.

———

"As to rape," mused Joe in cell 9,
"I'll take any cunt-hole for mine:
Dogs, sheep, mares, or squirrels,
Or if nothing else, girls—
As long as it screws, man, it's fine."

When Carol was told about sex,
She said, "Mother, it sounds so complex.
Do you mean you and father
Went through all that bother,
And I'm just the aftereffects?"

There once was a man named Steve,
Who always wanted to leave.
He went next door,
And found a whore,
And now when I see him, I heave.

A talking pussy—what a concept, my dear!
That's something I'd sure like to hear!
With my old lady's slot,
I can pump it a lot,
And it will give me a spirited cheer!

There was a young man named McFee,
Who was stung in the balls by a bee.
He made oodles of money
By oozing pure honey,
Every time he attempted to pee.

———

There once was a silly old widower,
Who wanted to dance to the fiddler.
With love in his heart,
He fell for the tart,
Who was the whole dancehall's free diddler.

———

There was an old hustler named Raines,
Possessed of more balls than of brains:
He stood on a stool,
To buttfuck a mule,
And got kicked in the nuts for his pains.

A hillbilly gent, name of Cato,
Wanted sex with his girl on a date-o.
She said, "Yer dick's real purdy,
But yer balls are too dirty,
They look like a fresh-dug potato."

———⁓⁓⁓———

'Cause the girl found no joy in her lap,
She chopped off her big brother's tap.
At his death, not repenting,
But fixed by cementing,
She wore it in place with a strap.

———⁓⁓⁓———

There once was a fellow named Simon,
Who for years couldn't pierce his wife's hymen,
'Til he hit on the trick,
Of sheathing his prick,
In a steel condom tipped with a diamond.

A newlywed couple called Goshen,
Spent their honeymoon sailing the ocean,
Through eighty positions,
Their complex coitions,
Demonstrated their fucking devotion.

—◦◦◦—

A young prostitute named Hortense,
Her usual fee is ten cents,
But she plays anyway,
When the fellow won't pay,
But it sure makes Hortense very tense.

—◦◦◦—

Young Jilly was feeling quite ill;
"What's the problem?" asked the doctor of Jill.
"I'm a veggie and use
For my pleasure just cues
And asparagus tips for a thrill."

There was a young man from D.C.,
Who went to the men's room to pee.
While acting the fool,
He pulled out his tool,
And pissed on himself and on me.

———

A man with a throbbing erection,
Who had forgotten to use protection,
Took a roll on the floor,
With a questionable whore,
And now has a nasty infection.

———

There once was a pervert named Mueller,
Who measured his dick with a ruler.
He found out his dong,
Was two inches long,
Then he turned off the lights so he'd fool her.

A singer, some called her a dyke,
She said, "No, I know what I like.
There aren't many men,
That give me a yen,
But, gee, I have fun with my mike."

———∾∾∾———

There was a young girl from Hoboken,
Who claimed that her hymen was broken,
From riding a bike
On a cobblestone spike,
But it really was broken from pokin'.

———∾∾∾———

There once was a lady called Pam,
Who took a short trip on a tram.
The fucking conductor
Took out his constructor,
And now she is wheeling a pram.

There once was a lady from Niger,
Who had an affair with a tiger.
The result of the fuck
Was a bald-headed duck,
Two gnats, and a circumcised spider.

There once was a well-blessed young Hindu,
Much admired in the towns that he'd been to,
By the women he knows
Who wriggle their toes
At the tricks he can make his foreskin do.

The widow McCree shopped for bread,
But bought a cucumber instead;
She told the store clerk,
"This damn thing should work,
It's endowed like my dead husband, Fred!"

There once was a man from Bel Air,
Who wanted to fuck a brown bear.
He pulled down his pants,
And began to romance,
Now he has just one ball and some hair.

—◦◦◦—

A libidinous justice from Salem,
Used to judge all the hookers and jail 'em.
But instead of a fine,
He would stand them in line,
With his common-law tool to impale 'em.

—◦◦◦—

There once was a man from Calcutta,
He jerked himself off in a gutter.
The tropical heat,
Affected his meat,
And instead of cream he got butter.

There was a soprano from Reggio,
Whose cunt was trained in solfeggio.
One day a contraction
Caused such a reaction,
She pissed, and missed an arpeggio!

———

There once was a man from Biarritz,
Who planted an acre of tits.
They came up in the fall,
Red nipples and all,
And he promptly chewed them to bits.

———

A young lass from North Carolina,
Had a most capricious vagina.
To startle the fucker,
It would suddenly pucker,
And whistle the chorus of "Dinah."

There once was a man from Boston,
Who drove a very nice Austin.
He had room for his ass,
And a tank full of gas,
But his balls hung out, so he lost 'em!

—∞—

Shrimpers in La Batre have the life;
A seaport town absent of strife.
A man came one day,
But he would not stay,
Said, "The sea here smells just like my wife!"

—∞—

There was a young lady, Miss Brent,
With a cunt of enormous extent.
'Twas so deep and so wide,
The acoustics inside
Were so good you could hear when you spent.

When they probed a young woman named Kannel,
Who complained she felt choked in her channel,
They found shoehorns and spoons,
Twelve busted balloons,
And twenty-two yards of red flannel.

—⁓—

There once was a whore on the dock.
From dusk until dawn she sucked cock.
'Til one day, it's said,
She gave so much head,
She exploded and whitewashed the block.

—⁓—

A certain old maid in Cohoes,
In despair taught her bird to propose;
But the parrot, dejected
At not being accepted,
Spoke some lines too profane to disclose.

There was a young man with the art
Of making a capital tart
With a handful of shit,
Some snot and a spit,
And he flavors the whole with a fart.

———

There was a young lady of Harriage,
Who said on the morn of her marriage,
"I shall sew my chemise
Right down to my knees,
For I'm damned if I'll fuck in the carriage!"

———

There was a young lady from Natchez,
Who was fully equipped with two snatches.
She often cried, "Shit!
I'd give up a tit
For a man with equipment that matches."

There once was a man from Kent,
Whose dick was so long it was bent.
To stay out of trouble,
He stuck it in double,
So instead of coming, he went.

A pox-ridden lady called Trix,
Was enamoured of sucking large pricks.
One fellow she took
Was a doctor called Crook,
Now he's in one hell of a fix.

An observant young man of the West
Said, "I've found out by personal test,
That men who make passes
At girls who wear glasses,
Get just as good sex as the rest."

A grubby young harlot called Schwartz
Had a cunt that was covered in warts.
They tickled so nice,
She'd command a high price,
From the blokes in the summer resorts.

—◈—

Young Jenny has dreams in her slumber,
Of dirtily dancing the rumba.
With veg like courgettes,
Real excited she gets,
'Til she comes to the cucumber number.

—◈—

A tuna fish salad for lunch,
On taco shells added for crunch,
Was more than just swell—
The sight, taste, and smell,
Brought thoughts of good times with Babs Bunch!

EVE

A sexy young woman called Eve,
Wore her pussy upon her left sleeve,
And her heart on the right
For doubled delight,
And something else you won't believe!

Her good friend Alonzo said, "Eve,
I am drawn to the scent of your sleeve.
May I kiss your left wrist?
Oh please? I insist!
It's the highest bliss I could achieve."

Said Eve to Alonzo, "You may
Kiss me first on the right and then play
Your tongue up and down
The left sleeve of my gown,
But make sure that you do it all day."

Said Alonzo to her, "Darling Eve,
All day long's far too short for your sleeve.
Is the rest of your life
(If you'll just be my wife)
Long enough? Otherwise I must leave."

Said Eve to Alonzo, "Please stay.
Both my sleeves say, 'Don't go away.'
You're melting my hips,
With the touch of your lips
On my sleeves. Please continue, I pray."

Said Alonzo, "I can't get enough,
And I'm charmed by this sweet little ruff—
So I shall, (by your leave)
Warm my face in your sleeve
As one warms one's hands in a muff."

Said Eve to Alonzo, "Sweet chap,
Leave my sleeve, come, and lie in my lap.
Though your ardor's not cooled,
I fear you've been fooled
By this poetic metaphor crap."

On doctor's strict orders I strove
To eat garlic each hour by the clove.
He said, "Good for the heart."
Well, it just made me fart,
But it saved on the gas for my stove.

———

A butcher, a baker, a candle-
Stick maker all wooed Mrs. Randall.
The butcher had meat
And the baker was sweet,
But 'twas candles she wanted to handle.

———

A miserly man named McEwan,
Inquired, "Why bother with screwin'?
It's safer and cleaner
To polish your wiener,
And besides, you can see what you're doin'."

Mother Superior to Head of the Garden
Said, "My nuns need a bit of a hard-on.
Nothing skinny or narrow,
But a squash like an arrow;
Nothing less will these randy girls pardon."

───∾∾∾───

There once was a dancer from Exeter,
So pretty that men craned their necks at her.
But some, more depraved,
Unzipped them and waved
The distinguishing marks of their sex at her.

───∾∾∾───

A caddy called Tommy the Tough
Had an heiress way out in the rough.
He said, "Let's not fuck,
Let's you and me suck."
And he buried his head in her muff.

SOAP OPERA

Anne went to a good plastic surgeon
To turn her back into a virgin.
In order to trick
A rich guy named Dick
To give in to her maternal urgin'.

Not only was Dick soon seduced,
The poor bastard was quickly reduced
To a married man's life,
With Anne as his wife,
And the fetus he thought he'd produced.

The real father, however, was Stan,
And here's a small flaw in Anne's plan:
Alas and alack!
Dick was white, Stan was black,
And the baby a rich shade of tan.

Was Dick in the least bit dismayed?
Not a bit! He just knelt down and prayed!
He blamed it on God,
'Stead of Stan's active rod,
And the role that the surgeon had played.

Now, you wonder how this will turn out?
What, in fact, the whole thing's all about?
Well, here's news for you,
I'm wondering, too,
And a clue without doubt I'm without!

There was a young bride named McWing,
Who thought sex a delirious fling.
When her bridegroom grew ill
From too much (as they will),
She found other men do the same thing.

———

There once was a being from Venus,
Who had a twenty-inch penis.
When day turned to night,
He thought, "It's all right,"
And wiped it off with a very large Kleenex.

———

There once was a woman called Dinah,
Who had an almighty vagina.
It wasn't the size
That attracted the flies,
But the traces of cum round the rim, ah.

There was an old abbess quite shocked.
She found nuns where the candles were locked.
Said the abbess, "You nuns
Should behave more like guns,
And never go off 'til you're cocked."

—∾—

"It's been a very fine day,"
Yawned Lady McDougal McKay.
"Three cherry tarts,
At least twenty farts,
Two shits, and a bloody good lay."

—∾—

There once was a girl, name of Joy,
Who couldn't find a good boy.
She'd get them all harried:
"No sex till we're married!"
So now she relies on a toy.

A juggling black cat named Pierre
Liked to walk with his tail in the air.
When the girl cats passed by,
They said, "My, oh my—
What a nice set of balls you have there."

There once was a man from Nantucket,
Whose dong was so long he could suck it.
He walked down the street,
Just swinging his meat,
While he carried his balls in a bucket.

There was a young man from Peru,
Who loved a fair maiden most true.
He said, "Do be mine."
She didn't decline,
So the couple was married at 2:00.

Some ladies have feminine arts,
That give to them musical parts.
Especially if humping
With doggy-style pumping,
They'll generate vaginal farts.

—◦◦◦—

A pansy who lived in Khartoum,
Took a lesbian up to his room,
And they argued all night
Over who had the right
To do what, with what, and to whom.

—◦◦◦—

I shared with a track star my hash,
But for sex she demanded hard cash.
We settled on price,
I was done in a trice,
She said, "You must sprint in the dash."

Jill stitched up a thing of soft leather,
And topped off the end with a feather.
When she poked it inside her,
She flew like a glider,
And gave up her lover forever.

———

Miss Vanderbilt screwed twenty goats,
(On their prowess she fervently dotes).
When she was through,
She had a cold brew,
And wrote them all nice thank-you notes.

———

"I don't use a candle for THAT!
It's waxy and slender and flat.
It'd melt and get gooey
The idea is too screwy!
You'd best put it back in your hat."

There was a fair maid named Anheuser,
Who said that no man could surprise her.
But Paul took a chance,
Found Schlitz in her pants,
And now she is sadder, Budweiser.

———∽∽∽———

An alluring but cranky au pair,
Was arrested for lethal child care—
The kid was a pain,
So she opened his vein,
But she swears that he tripped on a stair.

———∽∽∽———

A nudist resort in Bel Air,
Took a midget in unawares.
But he made members weep,
For he just couldn't keep,
His nose out of private affairs.

YOUNG MCBRIDE

There was a young man named McBride,
Who could fart whenever he tried.
At a contest he blew
Two thousand and two,
Then shit and was disqualified.

This same young fellow, McBride,
Preferred his trade long and wide;
But he never rejected,
Whatever erected,
For, "Peter is Peter," he sighed.

———

Karen was a generous hostess,
But the noise in her house went unnoticed.
My ears were pinned tightly,
Which was about nightly,
By legs which I wore like a poultice.

As Bradley is said to have said,
"If I think that I'm lying in bed
With this girl that I feel
And can touch, is it real,
Or just going on in my head?"

———

There was a boy scout from Kentucky,
Whose bottom was always kept bared. He
Explained, "The scoutmaster
Can enter me faster,
And a boy scout must be prepared, see?"

———

I had a small doggy named Lucky,
Who was just a horny old fucky.
Then one day he found
The neighbor's bloodhound,
And got his wee sausage quite stucky.

To his wife said Sir Hubert de Dawes,
"Fix this chastity belt round your drawers!"
But an amorous Celt
Found the key to the belt,
While the squire was away at the wars.

———

There once was a queer named Taylor,
Who seduced a very young sailor.
They threw him in jail,
But he worked out his bail,
By doing his thing on the jailor.

———

There was a young man from Bengal,
Who got in a hole in the wall.
"Oh," he said, "It's a pity
This hole is so shitty,
But it's better than nothing at all."

There once was a monk from Siberia,
Whose morals were somewhat inferior.
He did to a nun
What he shouldn't have done,
And now she's a mother superior.

———

When Theocritus guarded his flock,
He piped in the shade of a rock.
It is said that his muse,
Was one of the ewes,
With a twat like a pink hollyhock.

———

There was an old maiden named Grissing,
Who discovered what she had been missing.
She laid down with young Rod,
And cried out, "Oh, Dear God!
All these years I just used it for pissing."

The cheesemonger's daughter was fair,
Although he and his wife had black hair.
Was she his or the baker's,
The candlestick-maker's,
The butcher's, or Jim's with Gruyere?

—◦◦◦—

Jane met a young man for some action.
His foreplay gave her satisfaction.
They enjoined in coition,
In the strangest position,
And his femur is now up in traction.

—◦◦◦—

A frustrated young laundress of Lamas,
Would imagine great amorous dramas:
For the spots she espied,
Dried and hardened inside,
The pants of the vicar's pajamas.

A harlot from Harlem, so fine,
Used to peddle her ass all the time.
She first got ten bucks,
But she's down on her luck
So she'll fuck you for ten cents—or nine.

—

There once was a man named McSweeny,
Whose wife was a terrible meanie.
The hatch on her snatch
Had a catch that would latch,
And she only got fucked by Houdini.

—

There was a young lady called Blunt,
Who possessed a peculiar cunt.
She learned, for diversion,
Posterior perversion,
As no one could fit her in front.

THE CUNT

Seven smart men had some wine,
Then said, "It'd be real fine
To have for our bone,
Just a pussy alone..."
So they made a custom design.

First was a butcher with wit,
Who took a sharp knife from his kit,
Then with stylish precision,
He made an incision
And gave it a vertical slit.

Second, a carpenter bold,
Said, "Well, it's going to be poled."
So he took out his gimlet
And to a depth preset,
Made sure it was beautifully holed.

Third was a tailor quite thin,
Who said, "It would be such a sin
If it tended to scratch
While using this snatch..."
So he lined it with velvet within.

Fourth was a hunter quite stout,
Home from the hunt with a shout.
"I've got some fox fur
Just perfect for her!"
And lined it all softly without.

Fifth was a guy mean as hell,
An angler not thinking too well.
He said, "Well I like it!
So I will just spike it
With a fish to endow with that smell."

Sixth, a mild preacher, McGee,
Said, "For my usual fee
I'll touch it and bless it
(Might even caress it),
Then send it forth able to pee."

Last came a sailor, a runt,
Who took the thing out in a punt.
Firstly he sucked it,
Then of course fucked it,
And afterward coined the name "cunt."

The virile Virginia coal miner
Placed his eye near his girlfriend's vagina.
In the midst of the action,
With a mighty contraction,
She gave the fine miner a shiner.

———∽∽∽———

There was a young lad from Montana
Who had a fine wife, name of Hannah.
He could get no erection,
So in abject dejection,
He inserted a well-oiled banana.

———∽∽∽———

The queen of burlesque, Pussy Hunt,
Could whistle show tunes through her cunt.
But an investigation
Proved Pussy's vocation,
Was just a ventriloquist's stunt.

A possessive young fellow from Maine,
Tied his wife to the sink with a chain.
The chain soon was rusted,
The husband got busted,
Now communal showers mean pain!

———

There once was a lass from Samoa,
Who plugged up her cunt with a boa.
This weird contraceptive
Was very effective
To all but the spermatozoa.

———

There once was a man from Florida,
Who liked his friend's wife, so he borrowed her.
But when they got into bed,
He said, "May God strike me dead,
This isn't a cunt, it's a corridor!"

There once was a woman of Churston,
Who thought her third husband the worst one,
For he justly was reckoned
Far worse than the second,
And her second was worse than the first one.

———≈———

There was an old whore in Times Square,
Who went round with her genitals bare.
But the union said, "Stop!
You can't keep open shop.
We consider the practice unfair."

———≈———

There once was a farm boy named Nate,
Who yearned for a wonderful date.
When he ran out of luck,
He made do with a duck.
Said the priest, "Now they're husband and mate."

The wife of an absent dragoon
Begged a soldier to grant her a boon.
As she let down her drawers,
She said, "It's all yours—
I could deal with the whole damned platoon!"

———

There once was a guy called Reg,
Who fucked a girl in a hedge.
Then along came his wife
With a big carving knife
And cut off his meat and two veg.

———

A vagina, the organ of Venus,
Looks soft and inviting between us.
But that's enough looking,
Get on with the fucking,
Wishing fucking good luck to our genus.

There once was a fireman named Jerry,
Whose hose looked quite big, OH SO VERY!
His wife, she would pray
That his hose he would spray,
'Cause that would make her very merry.

———

There was a young man from Arras
Lying quiet and still on the grass.
With a sudden, huge lunge
He bent like a sponge,
And stuck his prick up his own ass.

———

There once was a man named Bob Brewster,
Who said to his wife as he goosed her,
"That used to be grand,
But just look at my hand,
You're not wiping as good as you used to."

There once was a man from New York,
Whose penis was shaped like a fork.
While screwing his wife,
Who was shaped like a knife
They could carve up a really nice pork.

———⟨∿∿⟩———

Said Kate, as she spread on the sand,
"I just hate to get sand in my gland,
For it tortures me scraping...
While I enjoy japing,
It's the sand in my gland I can't stand."

———⟨∿∿⟩———

There was a young lady named Slater,
Who married an old alligator.
The night that they wed
They climbed into bed,
But rather than mate her, he ate her.

There was a young lady from West Chester,
Who allowed all the men to molest her.
For a kiss and a squeeze
She would open her knees,
And she'd strip to the buff if they pressed her.

An avant-garde bard named McNamitar
Had a prick of prodigious diameter.
But it wasn't the size
That brought tears to their eyes,
'Twas the rhythm—iambic pentameter.

A self-centered fellow named Newcombe,
Who seduced many girls but made few come,
Said, "The pleasures of tail
Were ordained for the male.
I've had mine. Do I care if you get some?"

A childless man took to chasin'
A curvy young girl with elation.
She asked him, "Why me?"
He replied, full of glee,
"You were built for the birth of a nation!"

⟨∿∿⟩

I think she'll strike a nice pose,
Right there on the tip of my nose,
And give me a shot
Of her flower pot,
Then maybe I'll take off her clothes.

⟨∿∿⟩

The sight of a naked Michelle,
Snatch open with teeth sharp as hell,
Will mess up your sleep,
Making you weep,
And will stop wet dreams in one swoop fell.

My grandfather adored his old tether,
And loved tickling his balls with a feather.
But the thing he loved best,
Out of all of the rest,
Was jostling them gently together.

There once was a fellow in Maine,
Who sniffed and who snorted cocaine.
He was messed in the head,
And shot himself dead,
Which sent his dear wife quite insane.

The naked girls' choir down in Natchez,
Sing out, proudly showing their thatches,
And old deaf Bill Rose
Sneaks up very close,
To manage to catch a few snatches.

A clever old asshole called Frisk,
His method of screwing was brisk.
The idea was: "If
The bitch has the syph,
This way I'm reducing the risk."

———∿∿∿———

There was a boy who lived in the hay,
All he thought about was foreplay.
The sex was great,
But not his fate.
He decided, one day, to turn gay.

———∿∿∿———

There once was a woman named Alice,
Who pissed in the archbishop's chalice.
She later decreed
That she did it from need,
And not out of Protestant malice.

A tuna sat next to his brother.
Their dad looked from one to the other.
"Boys," he said, "listen,
Two things smell like fish, an'
Both of those things are your mother."

———

A sultan, inspecting his harem,
Said, "Eunuch, proceed to lay bare 'em."
Having seen the details,
He issued long veils,
And ordered the harem to wear 'em.

———

There was a young girl in the choir,
Who succumbed to her lover's desire.
She said, "It's a sin,
But now that it's in,
Could you shove it a few inches higher?"

There once was a lass from Gibraltar,
Whose purity a young man did alter,
But just as she came,
He reddened with shame,
For the strength of his manhood did falter.

———

There was a young girl whose divinity,
Preserved her in perfect virginity.
'Til a candle, her nemesis,
Caused parthenogenesis,
Now she thinks herself one of the Trinity.

———

There was an old man from China,
Who wasn't a very good climber.
He fell on a rock,
Split open his cock,
And now he's got a vagina.

There was a young lady named Mandal,
Who caused quite a neighborhood scandal,
By coming out bare,
In the village square,
And poking herself with a candle.

———

There was a young fellow called Howell,
Who pleasured himself with a trowel.
The triangular shape
Was conducive to rape,
But easily cleaned with a towel.

———

One day, making pickles with dill,
I found one that gave me a thrill.
It was ever so long,
And resembled a dong;
I've not used it yet, but I will.

There was a young maid from Madrid,
Wanted payment for sex, and most bid.
But a handsome Italian
With balls like a stallion
Said he'd do it for nothing—and did!

———

They tell of a lass named Regina,
Who said all's fine in Carolina,
But when I got there,
She was covered in hair,
Except for her shiny vagina.

———

An octogenarian Jew,
To his wife stayed steadfastly true.
'Twas not from compunction,
But due to dysfunction
Of his spermatic glands—nuts to you.

I wooed a lewd nude in Bermuda.
I was rude, but by God, she was ruder.
She said it was crude,
To be wooed in the nude.
I pursued her, subdued her, and screwed her.

———∿∿∿———

A young boy whose name was Kevin,
Used a vacuum to stretch it to seven,
Then eight and then nine,
And though ten was divine,
There'll be film when it reaches eleven.

———∿∿∿———

A worried young fellow, O'Doole,
Discovered red marks on his tool.
His doctor, a cynic,
Said, "Out of my clinic,
And wipe off that lipstick, you fool!"

A fair maid from Cairo called Nur,
Was thought quite incredibly pure,
'Til we saw her great stunt,
To ram up her cunt
A ton and a half of manure.

There once was a plumber from Lee,
Who was plumbing his girl by the sea.
She said, "Stop your plumbing,
There's somebody coming,"
Said the plumber, still plumbing—"It's me!"

There once was a fellow, McSweeny,
Who spilled some neat gin on his weenie.
Just to be couth,
He added vermouth,
Then slipped his girlfriend a martini.

A dominatrix, Madame Dale,
Liked to beat on her slaves with a flail,
Sayin', "Be lookin' cute,
While you're lickin' my boot,
And continue on up to my tail!"

———

There was a young lady from Brussels,
Who was proud of her vaginal muscles.
She could easily plex them,
And so interflex them,
As to whistle love songs through her bustles.

———

There once was a man from Bonaire,
Who was doing his wife on the stair.
When the banister broke,
He doubled his stroke,
And finished her off in midair.

A certain young chap named Bill Beebee
Was in love with a lady named Phoebe.
"But," said he, "I must see
What the clerical fee
Be, before she be Phoebe Beebee."

———

There're females in here in great number,
But most of them are in a slumber,
Or just simply jerkin',
Playing with a gherkin,
Banana, dildo, or cucumber.

———

A lonely old lady called May,
Used to stroll in the park 'cross the way.
There she met a young man
Who fucked her and ran—
Now she goes to the park every day.

Said a lesbian lady, "It's sad;
Of all of the girls that I've had,
None gave me the thrill
Of real rapture, until
I learned how to be a tribade."

———

An old hooker from West Tulsa cried,
"Had a twat once, incredibly wide.
You may think it banal,
But the Suez Canal
Was really quite tiny beside."

———

There was a young woman called Hall,
Wore a newspaper dress to a ball.
The dress caught on fire,
And burned her entire,
Front page, sports section, and all.

A young man whose sight was myopic,
Thought sex an incredible topic.
So poor were his eyes,
That despite its great size,
His penis appeared microscopic.

———

There was a young tart from South Bend,
Who tried lesbian sex with her friend.
With a moan and a grunt,
She licked her mate's cunt,
And loved it all right to the end.

———

There was a young lady called Hart,
Who felt that she needed to fart.
She stepped outside,
And to her surprise,
Blew over a horse and a cart.

Young Doris used lip balm with aloe,
But, mostly, it was made of tallow.
It said "Rub the wax
Into all of the cracks."
Now, Doris lies, frequently, fallow.

———

There once was an artist named Saint,
Who swallowed some samples of paint.
All shades of the spectrum,
Flowed out of his rectum,
With a colorful lack of restraint.

———

There's an oversexed lady named White,
Who insists on a dozen a night.
A fellow named Cheddar
Had the brashness to wed her—
His chance of survival is slight.

There was a young lady in Crew,
Whose cherry a chap had got through.
She told this to her mother,
Who fixed her another,
Out of rubber, red ink and some glue.

———

Old Louis Quatorze was 'ot steuff.
E tired of zat game, blindman's bleuff,
Upended his mistress,
Kissed 'ers as she kissed 'is,
And zo taught ze world *soixante-neuf*.

———

There was a young mister from Blister,
Who knocked up his girl as he kissed her,
But he couldn't afford,
A new baby on board,
So from then on he just had to fist her.

Weathergirl Angela Gore
Said, "Oh dear, it's really a bore.
When a cold weather front
Just blows up my cunt,
It makes it quite itchy and sore."

—◦◦◦—

There was a young gypsy called Rose,
With obsessions for gentlemen's hose,
Up her pussy, her rear,
In her mouth and each ear,
And her cute little freckle-tipped nose.

—◦◦◦—

There once was a gentleman, Mike,
Who met this chick he really liked.
He tried to get near,
But she gave him a sneer,
'Cause the chick was a fully fledged dyke.

YOUNG MARY'S CANARY

If you should go out with young Mary,
Take very great care, lads; be wary.
If you try to get in her,
She's got her own pecker—
Up her cunt she's stuffed a canary.

And should that canary go sniff,
And fall off its perch awful stiff,
With legs in the air,
Then you'd better beware
Of young Mary's obnoxious whiff.

———∞∞———

Pedro was a man in Peru,
Who fell asleep in his canoe.
While dreaming of Venus,
He played with his penis,
And woke up all covered with goo.

This woman I knew lived in Croft,
She played with herself in a loft,
Having reasoned that candles,
Could never cause scandals,
Besides which, they did not go soft.

———

There once was a monk from Kerplunks,
Whose body was that of a hunk's.
The nuns all went woozy
When in the Jacuzzi,
For the monk had forgotten his trunks.

———

A guy once existed named Stan,
Who had trouble being a man.
He wore dresses and heels,
Drove a car with pink wheels,
And eventually Stan was a tran.

On the tits of a barmaid from Sale,
Were tattooed all the prices of ale.
And on her behind,
For the sake of the blind,
Was the same list of prices in Braille.

———

A widow who lived in Rangoon,
Tied a black-ribbon wreath round her womb.
"To remind me," she said,
"Of my husband, who's dead,
And of what put him into his tomb."

———

There was a mean witch of the Rhone,
Who cursed an old harlot named Joan.
Not a man was amused,
Au contraire, they were bruised,
For they found she'd been plugged up with stone.

There once was this guy named Big Ward,
Whose girl was as flat as a board.
He'd suck as hard as he could,
Pull them more than he should,
But soon, even Ward, he got bored.

There once was a man from St. Paul,
Who swore he had only one ball.
Two dirty young bitches,
Tore down his breeches,
And found that he had none at all.

I had a good time with Miss June,
Yet told her to leave me, and soon.
We loved unencumbered,
Her days were all numbered;
Her puss now looks like a dried prune.

A soldier known only as Sarge,
Had sex with a hooker named Marge.
Though only a grunt,
He assaulted her cunt,
And gave her an honorable discharge.

———

So angular Jim got a spin
At Jodi's sweet vertical grin.
But the truth I must speak:
He likes 'em to squeak
With tightness while sliding it in.

———

There was a young man from St. Rose,
Whose love life was so full of woes,
He loved sixty-nine,
Like, all of the time,
But always got shit on his nose.

There was a young woman from Wheeling,
Bereft of all sexual feeling,
When a young man named Boris,
Did lick her clitoris,
He left her all legless and squealing.

Said an unhappy female named Sears,
"The world seems so full of those queers!
At the parties I go to
Are no men to say no to;
They swish about, wagging their rears."

There was a young man from Rangoon,
Who farted and filled a balloon.
The balloon went so high
That it stuck in the sky,
Which was tough for the Man in the Moon.

A versatile athlete called Grimmon,
Developed a new way of swimmin':
'Twas a marvelous trick,
He would row with his prick,
And attracted loud cheers from the women.

⸻

There was a young man from Natal
And Sue was the name of his gal.
He went out one day
For a rather long way—
In fact, right up Sue'z Canal.

⸻

The lady contortionist died,
When one day she foolishly tried
A difficult stunt,
With her head up her cunt,
Her nose caught on something inside.

A zoologist's daughter from Lansing,
Birthed a fine fritillary blue-wing.
Her father said, "Flo,
What I want to know
Isn't whether, but what, you've been screwing?"

———

There was an old geezer of Como,
Who suddenly cried, "*Ecce Homo*!"
He tracked his man down
To the heart of the town,
And gobbled him off in the Duomo.

———

A modest young maiden called Wilde
Sought to keep herself undefiled
By thinking of Jesus,
Contagious diseases,
And the bother of having a child.

There was a young lady of Dover,
Whose passion was such that it drove her
To cry when she came,
"Oh dear, what a shame!
Well, now we just have to start over."

———

A very young maid from Peru,
Had nothing whatever to do.
So she sat on the stairs,
And counted cunt hairs,
Five thousand, six hundred and two.

———

A rose is a rose is a rose,
I'm told, that's how the saying goes.
But if that sweet rose
Takes all Toms, Dicks, and Joes,
It soon won't smell sweet to this nose.

A Kentucky farmer named Kant,
His behavior was barely gallant,
For he fucked all his dozens
Of nieces and cousins,
In addition, of course, to his aunt.

—⁓—

There is a young woman from Venice,
A regular sexual menace—
For she'll hop from one boy
To another with joy,
Like the ball in a fast game of tennis.

—⁓—

The nipples of young Miss Hong Kong,
When excited were twelve inches long.
This embarrassed her lover
Who was pained to discover,
She expected no less of his dong.

I heard Vicky's moans on the air,
And I turned to the east just to stare.
And the scent the wind brang
Had a delightful tang,
And, oh, how I wished to be there!

—❧—

There was a young fellow from Datchet,
Who lopped off his prick with a hatchet.
He sent it to Whiteley,
With a note, wrote politely,
And ordered a cunt that would match it.

—❧—

I dislike all this crude notoriety
That I'm getting for my impropriety;
All that I ever do
Is what girls ask me to—
I admit, I get lots of variety.

This pretty pink meat doesn't smell
Like fish, so this thought please dispel.
She does take showers,
It smells like flowers,
'Cause she uses rose-scented hair gel.

———◦◦◦———

A preposterous King of Siam
Said, "For women I don't give a damn.
But a fat-bottomed boy
Is my glee and my joy—
They call me a pervert—I am!"

———◦◦◦———

There still is a whore from Des Moines,
Who, paid in advance, spreads her groin
To stash the full sum,
But if you don't come,
She'll pop out the change, bill and coin.

There once was a Cambridge B.A.,
Who pondered the problem all day
Of what there would be,
If c-u-n-t
Were divided by c-o-c-k.

⸻

When Dick met a young lady from Clare,
He was the very first one to get there.
She said, "Copulation
Can result in gestation,
But gosh, now you're here, I don't care."

⸻

There once was a golfer named Patch,
Whose tee shot went wide in a match.
It bounced in the crowd,
And a girl screamed aloud,
"That damn thing went right up my snatch!"

Said a co-ed from Duke University,
When asked about sexual perversity,
"I find it's okay
In the old-fashioned way,
But I do like a touch of diversity."

There was a young whore I call Mar,
Who once left my zipper ajar.
She left in a rush
While clutching her bush.
I hope her poor pussy don't scar.

There was a young lady from Dallas,
Who asked of her lover, "Just how is
It possible for you
To perform as you do?"
Said he, "Ability and prowess."

An ambitious young woman in Reno,
Lost most of her money on keno.
But she lay on her back
And opened her crack,
And now she owns all the casino.

———

There was a young fellow called Chubb,
Who joined a buttfucking club.
But his parts were so small,
He was no use at all,
And they promptly refunded his sub.

———

There was a young fellow from Trinity
Who ruined his sister's virginity,
Buttfucked his brother,
Had twins by his mother,
And took a degree in divinity.

An astonishing tribe are the Sweenies,
Renowned for the length of their weenies.
The hair on their balls
Sweeps the floors of their halls,
But they don't care for women, the meanies.

———

A lady from Morningside Crescent
Could never make men acquiescent
To a lewd proposition,
For they knew that coition
Wasn't safe with a cunt so putrescent.

———

Today's cinematic emporium
Is not just a visual sensorium,
But a highly effectual,
Heterosexual,
Mutual masturbatorium.

Since her baby came, Miss Snow
Won't diddle, she just hollers, "No!"
She thinks a fat senator
Was its likely progenitor,
But having laid ten she can't know.

———∽∽∽———

The girls who frequent picture palaces,
Care not for psychoanalysis.
They're rather annoyed
By the great Doctor Freud,
And cling to their long-standing phalluses.

———∽∽∽———

A novice, a priest fresh and green,
Was introduced to perversions obscene.
All manner of thuggery,
Rape, theft, and buggery,
Was committed by his Holiness the Dean.

A weakling who lacked protoplasm
Sought to give his young wife an orgasm;
But his tongue jumped the gap
From the front to the back,
And got pinched in a bad anal spasm.

———

A nearsighted fellow named Walter,
Led a glamorous lass to the altar;
A beauty he thought her,
'Til some soap and water
Made her look like the Rock of Gibraltar.

———

There was a young lady from Rheem,
Crept into the vestry unseen.
She ripped off her knickers,
Likewise the vicar's,
And rammed in the episcopal beam.

A circus midget named Pitts,
Was subject to passionate fits;
But his pleasure in life,
Was to suck off his wife
While he swung, by his knees, from her tits.

———

"Doc, I took your advice," said McKnop,
"And made the wife get up on top.
Got her bouncing about,
But it kept falling out,
And the kids, much amused, made us stop."

———

A pervert named Doctor Mark
Would take anything in the dark.
Be it bull or a vole,
He would proffer his hole,
And twice if it started to bark!

Now Caroline, writer of verse,
Was laid low one day by the curse.
And her menstrual flow
Was a bit of a blow,
To the laundress, who'd seen nothing worse.

———∾∾∾———

The sea captain's tender young bride,
Fell into the bay at low tide.
You could tell by her squeals,
That some of the eels
Had discovered a good place to hide.

———∾∾∾———

A toothsome young starlet named Smart
Was asked to display oral art.
As the price for a role,
She complied, met his goal,
Then sank her teeth into the part.

That explains the fact to me,
Despite flies and occasional fleas,
Why a small can of tuna
In a lesbian's bedroom-a
Is referred to as potpourri.

A mortician who practiced in Fife,
Made love to the corpse of his wife.
"How could I know, Judge?
She was cold, wouldn't budge,
Just the same as she acted in life."

An intrepid young Texan called Tom
Tried fucking while on a tandem.
At the peak of the make,
She slammed on the brake,
Spreading his semen at random.

I knew an old geezer named Caesar,
Who tried his darndest to please her.
Though overly stout,
And well-known as a lout,
He managed to tickle and tease her!

———

There was a young girl called Dawes,
Who went to a rave with no drawers.
Her mum said, "Amelia,
Should anyone feel ya
They'll think you're one of them whores."

———

A middle-aged hooker called Sandy,
Mistakenly drank too much brandy.
After ten glasses,
She let guys take passes,
Leaving them breathless and randy.

I once met a lady called Hester.
I took her back home and undressed her.
But I ran from the house
When I found that her mouth
Was riddled and starting to fester.

———

"At a séance," said a fellow called Post,
"I was being sucked off by a ghost;
Someone switched on the lights,
And there, in silk tights,
On his knees, was old Basil, my host."

———

A strapping fellow from Australia,
After his monthly bacchanalia,
Buttfucked a dog,
Three mice, and a frog,
And a bishop in fullest regalia.

There once was a man from Brighton,
Who said to his girl, "You're a tight one."
She said, "Pardon my soul,
But you're in the wrong hole;
There's plenty of room in the right one."

An elegant devil called Scott,
Took a busty young girl to his yacht.
Too lazy to rape her,
He made darts out of paper,
Which he languidly flew at her twat.

When a horny young curate in Leeds
Was discovered one day in the weeds,
Astride a young nun,
He cried, "Oh this is fun!
Much better than praying one's beads."

An admiral of old called Horatio
Was inordinately fond of fellatio.
He kept accurate track
Of the boys he'd attack,
And called it his cocksucking ratio.

———

There once was a fellow named Mitch,
With a dick that could dig a ditch!
He couldn't tell by their spasms
When ladies reached orgasms—
Only when their voices changed pitch!

———

There once was a girl (rather thick),
Who asked her Mom, "What's a dick?"
Mom said, "My dear Annie,
It goes up your fanny,
And jumps up and down 'til it's sick."

A nudist by the name of Fred Peet
Loved to dance in the snow and the sleet.
But one chilly December
He froze every member,
And retired to a monkish retreat.

⸻

A student who hailed from St. John's,
Badly wanted to buttfuck the swans.
"Oh, no," said the porter,
"Please buttfuck my daughter,
Them swans is reserved for the Dons."

⸻

There was a young man named Racine,
Who invented a fucking machine:
Concave and convex,
It would fit either sex,
With attachments for those in-between.

A disgusting young man called McGill,
Made his neighbors exceedingly ill
When they heard of his habits,
Involving white rabbits,
And a bird with a flexible bill.

———∞———

The bishop, one Sunday, at mass,
After eating a pound of spoiled bass,
Emitted a blast
That continued to last,
And extinguished the candles with gas.

———∞———

Sighed a newlywed bride of Wheeling,
"A honeymoon sounds so appealing,
But for nearly two weeks,
I've heard only bed squeaks
And seen nothing but cracks in the ceiling."

A tip for you jaded old souls:
Try changing the usual roles.
The backward position
Is nice for coition
And offers the choice of two holes.

Said a horrid old hag, "Look here, honey,
I know that I'm wrinkled and funny,
But get me in bed
With a sack on my head,
And I'll give you a run for your money."

There was a young man from St. Paul,
Who started his sleep in the fall.
But in hibernation
He tried masturbation;
It was better than nothing at all.

Cried the dumbfounded groom in despair,
"My pecker will never fit there!"
But his bride countered, "Hell,
It should fit very well,
And with plenty left over to spare."

———

A gentleman Katie knew slightly,
Persisted in calling her nightly,
To ask her if she
Would ever be free
To come by and tie him up tightly.

———

A remarkable race are the Persians,
They do have so many diversions.
They screw the whole day
In the regular way,
And save up the night for perversions.

There was a young fellow called Lancelot,
Whose neighbors looked on him askance a lot.
Whenever he'd pass
A pretty young lass,
The front of his pants would advance a lot.

———

Little Emily's blonde and attractive
And extremely sexually proactive.
Her tight little twat
Has grown so red hot
That the damn thing is radioactive.

———

A young friend of mine, name of Kemball,
Looked just like a large phallic symbol.
The top of his head
Was round, shiny, and red—
When he walked he made women tremble.

There was a young lady from Norway,
Who hung by her heels from a doorway.
She said to her beau,
"Hey, look at this, Joe,
I think I've discovered one more way!"

———∽∾∽———

When the judge with his wife having sport,
Proved suddenly two inches short,
The good lady declined,
And the judge had her fined
By proving contempt of his court.

———∽∾∽———

The Vicar of Dunstan St. Just,
Consumed with irregular lust,
Raped the Bishop's prize fowls,
Buttfucked four shocked owls,
And a little green lizard that bust.

I never will finish with Mandy,
She's sweeter than apricot brandy.
Her tight little crack
Means I cannot hold back;
My cock in her cunt feels too dandy.

———

There once was a big boy called Bowen
Whose penis kept growin' and growin'.
It grew so tremendous,
So heavy and pendulous,
'Twas no good for fuckin'—just showin'.

———

When Milton inspected his willy,
He said, "It's so short, it's just silly.
It's becoming so small,
I can't find it at all,
And I soon won't be Milt, I'll be Millie."

My wife is an amorous soul,
On fire for a young athlete's pole.
She called her chauffeur
Her sexual gopher,
And, boy, did he go for her hole!

—∿∿—

A handsome young stud from Purdue,
Who was only just learning to screw,
Found he hadn't the knack,
He was much too far back—
It was the right church, but wrong pew.

—∿∿—

"Oh gosh!" said young Rita from Harrow,
"Your penis is huge, that's so rare-o."
"Not quite," said her school
Teacher, wielding his tool,
"It's your cunt that's exceedingly narrow."

A wife who was all aggravation
Left on a permanent vacation.
Her husband stayed home
With his joystick, alone,
And spent nights with his Sony Playstation.

———

There was a young lady named Myrtle
Who had an affair with a turtle.
She had crabs, so they say,
In a year and a day,
Which proves that the turtle was fertile.

———

A neurotic young man of Kildare,
Drilled a hole in the seat of a chair.
He fucked it all night,
Then died of the fright
That maybe he wasn't "all there."

There was a young lady named Sharkie,
Who had an affair with a darkie.
The result of her sins
Was quads—not just twins—
One white, and one black, and two khaki.

———∾∾∾———

A lewd Northumbrian Druid
Had a mind so filthy and crude.
He woke from a trance,
With his hand in his pants,
On a patch of cold seminal fluid.

———∾∾∾———

There was a young stud from Missouri
Who fucked with astonishing fury,
'Til taken to court
For his vigorous sport,
And condemned by a poorly hung jury.

To a whore, said the cold Lady Dizzit,
"Lord D's a new man since your visit.
As a rule, the damned fool
Can't erect his old tool—
You must have what it takes, but what is it?"

———

Miss Fanny, adored by John Keats,
Loved romance and sucking on sweets;
Yet one glance from this skirt
Could reduce the poor squirt
To a few inarticulate bleats.

———

There was a young man from Majorca,
Whose bird was an absolute corker.
Her curvaceous figure
Filled him with vigor
And thrills as he managed to pork her.

The snatch of a waitress named Pips,
Bottomed out just an inch past the lips.
Though her muff was not deep,
She cried not a peep,
'Cause she made a good living on tips!

A lady encountered two vicars
Who attempted to take off her knickers.
When she remonstrated
They replied, quite elated,
"Blame it all on spirituous liquors!"

An unfortunate chap from Hyde,
Once fell down a toilet and died.
His unhappy mother,
She fell down another;
Now they're interred side by side.

WILLIAM'S WARNING

Say I to thee, dearest, beware
Of men like me who to thee fair
Wilt give thee a rose
Whilst shedding our clothes
For more than our souls doth we bare.

But should thy fair hand reach to pick
Thy rose, dear, thou mustn't be quick
To pluck, else in kind,
Thou wilt surely find
In thy tenderest fingers a prick.

—⦿—

"Last night," said a lady called Ruth,
"In a long-distance telephone booth,
I enjoyed the perfection
Of an ideal connection—
I was screwed, if you must know the truth."

There was a young sailor named Xavier,
Who cared not for God, nor his savior.
He walked on the decks,
Displaying his sex,
And was stopped for indecent behavior.

———

There was an old pervert named Tucker,
When instructing a novice cocksucker,
Said, "Don't stretch out your lips
Like an elephant's hips—
We men like it best if you pucker."

———

I have serviced this town now for years,
Since the days when the gays were just queers.
I gave most of the gentry,
Their very first entry,
And now all I hear are their jeers.

A beautiful girl was Hortense;
The size of her breasts were immense.
One day playing soccer,
Out popped her left knocker—
She kicked it right over the fence!

———

An attractive young girl from Des Moines
Had a very large sack full of coins—
The nickels and dimes
She had earned from the times
That she cradled young lads in her loins.

———

There was a young lady, Miss Clau,
Who said that she didn't know how.
Then a young fellow caught her
And jolly well taught her,
And she can't have enough of it now.

There once was a man from Iran,
Who fried both his nuts in a pan.
He said with a shout,
"PUT THE DAMN FIRE OUT!
Just as fast as you possibly can!"

———

"Yes, of course," said a girl from Lathrop,
"But it's hard to know quite where to stop…
A boy lifts your slip,
You hear him unzip—
Then what do you do, call a cop?"

———

There was a young fellow of Wadham,
Who asked for a ticket to Sodom.
When they said, "We prefer
Not to issue them, sir."
He said, "Don't call me sir! Call me madam."

A dentist living up on the hill,
Was a demon when it came to the drill.
But instead of the mouth,
He would place it due south,
After knocking them out with a pill.

———

An innocent maiden from Maine
Declared she'd a man on the brain.
But you knew from the view
Of the way her waist grew,
It was not on her brain he had lain.

———

There was a young couple called Kelly
Who had to live belly to belly,
For once, in their haste,
They used library paste
Instead of petroleum jelly.

There was a young lady, Miss Smith,
Whose virtue was mostly a myth.
She said, "Try as I can,
I can't find a man
Whom it's fun to be virtuous with."

———

While ogling a statue of Venus,
A man started rubbing his penis:
"She don't need no arms,
To show me her charms."
(They're dirty pricks, museum cleaners.)

———

There once was a man named John Wyatt,
Whose sexual likes were a riot.
From horses to hens,
To mice and to men,
If it had a hole, he would try it.

A flaccid young fellow called Spiff,
Spent February wondering if
He spent all of March
With his dick soaked in starch,
In April it might get more stiff.

———

A young man with passions quite gingery
Tore a hole in his sister's best lingerie.
He spanked her behind
And made up his mind
To add incest to insult and injury.

———

Now you've gotten that off of your chest,
You may think that your pussy's the best,
But it's only a sheath
And unless it has teeth,
It's no different from all of the rest.

A young lady was fond of a stunt,
So she took off her clothes in a punt.
She uncorked some champagne
And without any shame
She sprayed it all over her front.

—⟋∿∿⟍—

Winter is here—it's a grouch.
It's a time when you sneeze and you slouch.
You can't take your women
Out canoein' or swimmin'
But there's lots you can do on the couch!

—⟋∿∿⟍—

A dyslexic whore named Yvette,
Thought she'd drum up some trade on the net.
But gash, ckus, and ckuf
Made her role sound so rough
The SM-ers are all she can get.

A group of blind lesbians were bunchin'
Together to have a big luncheon.
But no one could tell,
Except by the smell,
Exactly whose cunt each was munchin'!

———⟋⟋⟋———

There once was a man from Lancaster
Who, while eating, befell a disaster.
His bowels, well-loaded,
Swelled up and exploded,
And filled his nice knickers with plaster.

———⟋⟋⟋———

An old couple at Eastertide
Were having fun sex when he died.
The wife for a week
Sat tight on his peak,
And bounced up and down as she cried.

There was a young man of Cape Cod,
Who into my wife put his rod.
His name, it was Tucker,
The dirty li'l fucker,
The bastard, the sucker, the fraud!

An abbot in the town of Brittany,
Once chanted this desolate litany:
"If Christ is the source
Of divine intercourse,
Then how come I don't ever get any?"

There once was a young man called Denzil
Whose organ was shaped like a pencil.
Anemic, it's true,
But an excellent screw,
Inasmuch as the tip was prehensile.

There once was a man from Nantucket,
Who was fucking a pig in a bucket.
The pig said with a grunt,
"That's my ass, not my cunt.
Come around to the front and I'll suck it."

———

There was a young fellow named Paul,
Couldn't rely on his toilet at all.
When he sat on the loo,
It went slightly askew,
And splattered some poop on the wall.

———

A lady from Dallas, so fair!
Had five large breasts and seven small spares.
There were four in a line,
The effect was divine,
While the others were formed up in squares.

There was an inventor named Tucker,
Who built a vagina of yucca,
But his words were obscene,
When the fractious machine,
Got a grip and refused to unpucker.

＊＊＊

In summer he said she was fair,
In autumn her charms were still there.
But he said to his wife,
In the winter of life,
"There's no spring in your old derriere."

＊＊＊

An ancient but jolly old bloke
Once picked up a young lass for a poke;
He wore her plum out
With his fucking about,
Then he shit in her shoe for a joke.

Said a diffident lady named Jude,
The first time she saw a man nude,
"I'm glad I'm the sex
That's concave not convex,
For I don't fancy things that protrude."

———≈———

A Sunday school student in mass
Soon rose to the top of the class,
By getting things right,
And sleeping the night
With his tongue up the clergyman's ass.

———≈———

As she knelt on her knees in prayer,
Sue felt something hard under there.
Good old Brother Bub
With his cane gave a rub
To her snatch, oh yes, it was bare!

There was a young fellow named Perkin
Who was always jerkin' his gherkin.
His father said, "Perkin,
Stop jerkin' your gherkin—
Your gherkin's for ferkin' not jerkin'!"

———∾∾∾———

She wanted to grow up a saint,
And her mother, she had no complaint,
But men—quite a few,
Were more fun than a pew,
So she wanted to be, but she ain't!

———∾∾∾———

I've been fitted with bionic sheath!
You can feel it in here, underneath.
It's programmed to snap
And to wrap and entrap,
And to nibble with its tiny teeth!

An unfortunate pirate called Bates,
Liked to do the fandango on skates.
But he fell on his cutlass,
Which rendered him nutless,
And practically useless on dates.

A lexicographer known as Boris,
Was fondling his sweetheart's clitoris.
He said, "No words have I
To describe such hair pie.
For that I will need my thesaurus."

A sailor who once lived in Briggen,
Went to sea to recover from frigging.
But after a week,
As they climbed the forepeak,
He buttfucked his mate in the rigging.

There was an old man of the isles,
Who suffered severely from piles.
He couldn't sit down,
Without a deep frown,
So he had to row standing—for miles!

Brigitte, who was from France,
Performed a peculiar dance.
She twirled all around,
Her panties fell down,
And gave all the boys a quick glance!

A certain young bride from Key West,
Was uncommonly large in the chest.
Her man's close attention
To her outsize dimension
Made his own dick measure its best.

A sultan who likes his girls buxom
At ninety still often abducts 'em
And then they are led
To a sumptuous bed
In which he regretfully tucks 'em.

———

There was a young girl from Rabat,
Who had triplets: Nat, Pat, and Tat.
It was fun in the breeding,
But hell in the feeding,
When she found she had no tit for Tat.

———

There once was a girl from New York,
Whose vagina was plugged with a cork.
To remove it, she fingered,
But still the cork lingered,
So she got it all out with a fork.

Melissa has shaved off the fringe
Of small curls that surrounded her minge.
But it's far from delightful
And looks pretty frightful;
Not somewhere I'd put my syringe.

———

In spite of a fearsome disease,
O'Reilly went down on his knees
Before altars of gods,
Whores, boys, and large dogs—
And all this for very small fees.

———

A hot-blooded Spaniard named Neal
Made all his young servants reveal
Their parted pudenda
In his hacienda,
Then promptly would screw them with zeal!

A bather whose clothing was strewed,
By winds that left her quite nude,
Saw a man come along,
And unless we are wrong,
You expected this line to be lewd.

———

A lesbian lady named Annie,
Wished to be less girly, more manly,
So she whittled a pud
Of gnarly old wood,
And let it protrude from her cranny.

———

Said a pretty young whore of Hong Kong,
To a long-pronged patron named Wong,
"They say my vagina
Is the best one in China,
Don't ruin it by donging it wrong!"

A considerate fellow named Tunney
Had a whizzer well worth any money.
When eased in halfway,
The girl's sigh made him say,
"Why the sigh?" "For the rest of it, honey."

———

Well-buttfucked was a boy named Kass
By all of the boys in his class.
He said, with a yawn,
"Now the novelty's gone,
It's only a pain in the ass."

———

The spouse of a pretty young thing
Came home from the war in the spring.
He was lame, but he came
With his dame like a flame—
A discharge is a wonderful thing.

Sue said to her neighbor's young son,
"Would you take my dog, Rex, for a run?"
He said, "Any day
With your dog I would play;
With your pussy I'd have much more fun."

Long ago once in ancient Japan,
Was a geisha who dressed as a man.
Her pants were so tight
That they rubbed her just right,
When she walked you might say that she ran.

A man bought a sexual device
And tried the thing out once or twice.
But it wasn't the gong,
But rather his prong,
That vibrated and didn't feel nice.

A forward young man with a fiddle
Asked a young fan, "Do you diddle?"
She replied, "Yes, I do,
But prefer it with two—
It's twice as much fun in the middle."

———

A man who was not very kind,
Used his penis instead of his mind.
One day he bent over,
So his dog could take over,
And give him a bone from behind.

———

There was a young man from Coblenz,
Whose balls were quite simply immense:
It took forty draymen,
A priest, and three laymen,
To transport them thither and hence.

There was a most versatile whore,
As expert behind as before.
For five bucks you could view her,
And buttfuck and screw her,
While she stood on her head on the floor.

———

Mighty proud of her snatch was Miss Latchett—
For hours she would just sit and scratch it.
She'd say with a smile,
"It has tone, it has style;
There ain't many snatches to match it."

———

The desperate Vicar of Goring
Drilled a suitable hole in the flooring.
He lined it all 'round,
Then gently he ground.
It's neater and cheaper than whoring.

An elderly gent from Tagore
Wished to try out his cook as a whore.
He used Bridget's twidget
To fidget his digit,
And now she won't cook anymore.

———⟨∞⟩———

A comely masseuse known as Nancy,
Was struck by a lewd passing fancy.
She lubed up with hot oil,
Brought herself to a boil,
All the while she was wearing no pant-sy.

———⟨∞⟩———

Said a woman with open delight,
"My pubic hair's perfectly white.
I admit there's a glare,
But the fellows don't care.
They can find it more quickly at night."

The man from Brazil was so weird.
His friends said, "It's perfectly clear.
He has a big dong
That he cleans all day long
By rubbing it on his long beard!"

—⟨⟩—

There once was a matron of Ottawa,
Whose husband, she said, thought a lot of her.
Which, to give him his due,
Was probably true,
Since he'd sired twenty kids, all begot on her.

—⟨⟩—

A loopy young fellow from Mecca,
Discovered a record from Decca,
Which he spun on his thumb
(These eccentrics are dumb),
While he needled the disc with his pec-a.

My mother lay there in great strain.
She bore me—it gave me great pain.
I looked at that tunnel,
That sure was no fun, hell,
I'm not going up there again.

—◦◦◦—

"Well, Madam," the Bishop declared,
While the Vicar just mumbled and stared.
'Twere better, perhaps,
In the crypt or the apse,
Because sex in the nave must be shared."

—◦◦◦—

A lad of extremely high station,
Was found by a prudish relation
Making love in a ditch
To—I won't say a bitch—
But a woman of "no reputation."

There was a young virgin called Fyffe
Who married the love of his life.
But imagine his pain
When he struggled in vain,
And just couldn't enter his wife.

—∾∾—

"My nieces are darling," said Sid.
"To oblige them, I do as I'm bid."
As he tucked them in bed,
He asked, "What's to be read?"
"Uncle Rhemus!" they cried. (And he did.)

—∾∾—

There was a señora from Spain
Whose appearance was mighty plain,
But her lips had a pucker
That made the men fuck her,
Again and again and again.

A pathetic appellant in Reno
Was as chaste as the Holy Bambino,
For she'd married a slicker
Who much preferred liquor
Over her ripe maraschino.

—⟐—

My eyes are deceiving me now—
My captain, he stands in the prow.
His ship has returned,
The aliens spurned,
And soon he will fart like a cow!

—⟐—

A blind date, my friend did devise.
He assured me a pleasant surprise.
When the time came to meet
I was startled to greet
A nice girl with blue tits and big eyes.

The general commanding Fort Totten
Had a habit both snobbish and rotten—
He made men of high ranks
Open left and right flanks
While their privates were mostly forgotten.

———ᔕᔕᔕ———

Have you heard that young Jimmy McGuire
Had an alcohol-fueled desire?
To meet a maid who'd give head,
And he'd lick her sweet spread—
Then he'd feel like a real vampire!

———ᔕᔕᔕ———

On the talk show last night, Dr. Ellis
(The sex shrink) took two hours to tell us,
"It's all right to enjoy
A rosy-cheeked boy—
So long as your sheep don't get jealous."

A girl that I met in the Louvre
Had the warmest vagina that you've
Ever dreamed of—unique,
And so tight, it would squeak,
When slipping my tongue in her groove.

———

"There surely must be a trick to it,"
Said a Peeping Tom watching all through it.
"While he's locked in that ring,
I will whip out my thing,
And polish it while I review it."

———

There was a young fellow named Stu,
Whose tool was so straight and so true,
That the navy, when fighting,
Could use it for sighting;
At one mile it could sink a canoe.

I'm amazed what technology brings,
And how inventors come up with new things.
Who would have guessed it,
Or would even suggest it,
That a tampon would—one day—have wings?

A worn-out old hooker called Tupps
Was heard to confess in her cups:
"The height of my folly
Was fucking a collie,
But I got a fine price for the pups."

There was a small woman called Sparrow,
Who complained that her cunt was too narrow.
For times without number,
She would use a cucumber,
But could not insert a man's marrow.

The farmer's oldest daughter once lay
With her legs wide apart in the hay;
Then, calling a plowman,
She said, "Do it now, man!
Don't wait 'til your hair has turned gray!"

In a town by the bay lived a fool,
Who kept his long tool on a spool.
One cold night it unraveled,
To a convent it traveled
And was promptly chopped up as a Yule.

A newlywed bride, Mrs. Young,
Asked the doctor to fix her torn lung.
When asked how it ripped,
She replied as she stripped,
"That man that I married is hung."

An unusual woman called Creek
Had taught her vagina to speak.
It was frequently liable
To quote from the Bible,
But when fucking—not even a squeak!

———

There once was a lady from Kos,
Who was fucking a man just because.
From her cunt fell a brick,
He yelled, "Girl, are you sick?"
She said, "No, but the guy before was."

———

Said a very attractive young Haitian,
"Please begin with a gentle palpation.
If you do as I say
In the way of foreplay,
Why, who knows? There could be fornication."

The things that occur on the shingle
Of the beaches surrounding old Dingle
Can only be said
In the bed of the wed
'Cause they'd tingle the single to mingle!

———

There was a young woman with blisters,
By far more willing than her sister.
The sister would giggle,
And wriggle and jiggle,
But this one would come if you kissed her.

———

There once was a fart deep within,
That thought to stay in was a sin.
So it tunneled about,
'Til it found its way out,
As I silently sat with a grin.

BATH TIME

Oh, Peter, my darling delight,
I've had no fun whatsoever tonight.
I'm feeling awry.
My panties are dry.
Please come and set me a-right.

I'm here in the bath, by the way.
(Waiting for you to come and to play.)
I've filled it, you see
With bubbly Chablis
For it's coq au vin *je voudrais*.

Hi Petal, I'm back! (With a bone!)
(Do I hear them all say with a groan,
"Oh my god—not again,
Has he sex on the brain?")
I'll make sure you're not bathing alone.

Now Chardonnay, Soave, and Chablis
With bubbles do wonders for me.
They perk up my stalk
'Til I'm popping my cork.
Even better's Champagne … you agree?

I bet it's the bubbles which get
You incredibly wanton and wet,
As gently they settle
And burst on your petal—
Just the thought of it's making me sweat.

You want me to come around and play?
I'll be there with no further delay!
If you're still hot and damp
You'll relieve me my cramp
That I've suffered for much of the day.

A newlywed husband named Jim
Asked his bride if she'd "sixty-nine" him.
When she just shook her head,
He sighed, and then said,
"Well, if we can't lick 'em, let's join 'em."

———༄༅———

An old professor named Bryce,
Dabbled in all sorts of vice.
He loved virgins and boys,
And mechanical toys,
And on Mondays, he meddled with mice.

———༄༅———

I once knew a waitress named Robyn.
Every night her bed was a bobbin'.
The men would take leave
After being quite pleased
And leave Robyn's fair body a-throbbin'.

There was a young virgin from Devon,
Who was raped in the garden by seven
High Anglican priests—
The lascivious beasts—
It wasn't the Kingdom of Heaven.

—◦◦◦—

It seems that all our perversions
Were known to the Greeks and the Persians.
But the French and the Yanks
Earn undying thanks
For inventing some modernized versions.

—◦◦◦—

"Big breaths," said the good Doctor Sung.
As his stethoscope tested her lung.
In all likelihood,
She misunderstood:
"Yeth, I've had them thince I was quite young."

My boy, if you like to have fun—
Just take all the girls one-by-one
And, when reaching four score,
Still you don't find it a bore—
Why then, you're a hero, my son.

———

On a date with a charming young bird,
His erotic emotions were stirred.
So with bold virile pluck,
He inquired, "Do you fuck?"
She said, "Yes, but please don't use that word."

———

There was a young man from Atlantis,
Who took off an Amazon's panties
And took her to bed
Where she cut off his head
But he carried on, just like a mantis.

Here's the tale of a chef from France,
Who was a victim of drunk circumstance…
Though he burned the baguette,
What he lived to regret,
Was the loaf that he pinched in his pants.

———

As a nurse was staring at the ceiling,
Her lover before her was kneeling.
Said she, "Dearest Hunt,
Take your hand off my cunt—
I much prefer fucking to feeling."

———

The nice girls, they say, love a candle,
Whenever they've no man to handle.
But that Roman kind
May well blow their mind,
Or else burn their cunt—what a scandal!

There once was a warden of Wadham,
Who approved of the folkways of Sodom.
"For a man might," he said,
"Have a very poor head,
But be a fine fellow, at bottom."

One evening, with forethought and malice,
A horny girl traveled to Dallas.
She liked to play cowboy,
Saying, "Hey, you, be my boy,
Just bring on the whips and your phallus!"

A hapless young laddie from Poole
Had a nut on the end of his tool.
When he went to unscrew it
His Pa said, "Don't do it,
Or your ass will fall off, you young fool!"

A geologist named Doctor Rob,
Was perturbed by the urge in his knob.
So he put down his pick
And jerked off his stick,
Then calmly went on with his job.

———

An astronomer, pious but odd
(To be honest, a dirty old sod),
Who'd searched for a sign
Of the presence divine,
Cried, "I've just found Uranus, dear God!"

———

Well, better I just keep mum, huh?
'Bout why it's so large when you slumber.
You are but a fake,
And it was a mistake;
It's naught but a whopping cucumber!

The coroner reported in Preston,
"The verdict is anal congestion.
I found an eight ball
On a sailmaker's awl
Halfway up the commander's intestine."

———

A young lady with dubious style,
Liked to take off her clothes for a while.
She'd get down on her knees,
And mainly to please,
She'd show off her vertical smile.

———

An elderly bishop from the West,
Quite openly practiced incest.
"My sisters and nieces
Are all dandy pieces,
And don't cost a cent," he confessed.

Bill, from Arkansas, U.S. president,
While in the White House, resident,
Did his staff of office display,
In a most unusual way,
Then claimed it was JFK's precedent.

—⚬⚬⚬—

A cruel old whore from Albania
Hated men with a terrible mania.
With a clench and a squirm
She would pinch back the sperm,
Then roll on her front and disdain ya.

—⚬⚬⚬—

Said a man to a lady of sin,
As he peeked up her dress with a grin,
"I came out of a spot,
Just like that, but *mein Gott!*
With yours, I could crawl right back in!"

There was a young lady called Ransom,
Who was serviced three times in a hansom.
When she cried, "Give me more!"
A voice from the floor
Said, "My name is Simpson not Samson."

—◦◦◦—

A young trapeze artist named Bract
Is faced by a very sad fact:
Imagine his pain,
When, again and again,
He catches his wife in the act!

—◦◦◦—

A pretty virgin called Miss Temple,
Had sexual parts so simple—
On peeking they found,
Little more than a mound,
In the center of which was a dimple.

More research is needed, I feel.
So ladies, please say how you'd deal,
With a bottle of Coke
Shaken first by a bloke
in panties. Does this appeal?

—∿∿—

There once was a sensitive bride,
Who ran when the groom she espied.
When she saw his cock stout
She almost passed out,
But when he got it in, she just sighed.

—∿∿—

There was an old man called Houdini,
From out of his pants came his weenie.
He tried at her dent
But when his thing bent,
He got down and used a zucchini.

With his penis in turgid erection,
And aimed at a woman's midsection,
Man looks most uncouth,
In that moment of truth,
But she receives it with loving affection.

———

There once was a cook in a kitchen,
Who couldn't stop howlin' and bitchin'.
She claimed Aunt Jemima
Had stole her vagina,
And shut it up tight with some stitchin'.

———

There was a young girl from Cornell,
Whose nipples were shaped like a bell.
When you touched them, they shrunk,
But when she got drunk,
They quickly got bigger than hell.

A convict, once, out in Australia,
Said unto his turnkey, "I'll tail ya."
But he said, "You be buggered,
You filthy old sluggard,
You're forgetting that I am your jailor."

—◦◦◦—

An agreeable girl called Miss Doves
Likes to fondle the young men she loves.
She will use her bare fist
If the fellows insist
But she really prefers to wear gloves.

—◦◦◦—

She told him, "With me, please don't mess,
Just now I am under great stress."
The rash youth persisted,
'Til he no longer existed,
And the moral? Beware P.M.S.!

An astonished ex-virgin named Howard
Remarked, after being deflowered,
"I knew that connection
Was made in that section,
But not that it's so darn high-powered."

—⟋∾⟍—

A soldier who was in the Alliance,
Fucked his own ass in defiance,
Not only of habit
And morals but—damn it!—
Most of the known laws of science.

—⟋∾⟍—

"Remember that lady from Venus,
Whose body fit nicely between us?"
Said Barney to Fred,
"She sure gave nice head,
But her tooth-laden twat hurt my penis!"

A neurotic young playboy named Gleason
Liked boys for no tangible reason.
A frontal lobotomy
Cured him of sodomy,
But ruined his plans for the season.

———

A complacent old Don of Divinity
Made boast of his daughter's virginity.
They must have been dawdlin'
Down at old Magdalen
It couldn't have happened at Trinity.

———

When a woman in strapless attire
Found her breasts lifting higher and higher,
The guests formed a line
For the mantle was fine
And they all wished to stoke up the fire.

There once was a butcher from Clack,
Who found slicing meat was his knack,
Up until the day
He met his "friend" Ray.
Now he only takes meat in the back.

———

There was a young girl named Priscilla,
Who flavored her cunt with vanilla.
The taste was so fine,
Men and beasts stood in line,
But she called it a day with Godzilla.

———

Your steel balls collide with my shell
And ring like the clock tower bell!
My scabbard of steel
Is starting to feel
Quite warm … Ooh! Now it's hot as hell!

There was a young fellow named Keating,
Whose pride took a terrible beating.
That happens to males
When they learn the details
Of their wives' extramarital cheating.

―〰―

There once was a fellow named Roy,
Who inserted a rather large toy.
He couldn't believe it
When he went to retrieve it,
For he pulled out two men and a boy.

―〰―

"I wouldn't be bothered with drawers."
Says one of our better-known whores:
"There isn't much doubt
I'd do better without
In handling my everyday chores."

There was an old lady in diapers,
Who got shot in the ass by some snipers,
And when she blew air
Through the holes that were there,
She astonished the old Irish pipers.

———

A suspicious old man in his car,
To his wife said, "How fat in front you are.
You have not been imprudent,
I hope, with some student?"
She said, "Really, now you're going too far!"

———

There once was a girl from Carolina,
Who possessed an enormous vagina.
Once while masturbating,
Lost her ring, how frustrating,
Went to get it, and now we can't find 'er.

A fellow with an unusual goal
Had a torrid affair with a mole.
Though surely a nancy,
He did rather fancy
Himself in the dominant role.

A highly bored damsel called Brown,
Remarked as she laid herself down:
"I hate to be doing
This promiscuous screwing,
But what else can you do in this town?"

There once was a minister named Jim,
Whose body was exceedingly thin.
As he whipped out his missile,
His new bride did whistle,
'Til he thrust in up to her chin.

There was a young girl called McBight,
Who got drunk with her boyfriend one night.
She came to her bed
With a split maidenhead
'Twas the last time she ever got tight.

————

The passengers all were delighted,
The stewardesses, too, were excited;
Up there in the void,
They really enjoyed
The pleasure of flying United!

————

There was a young woman called Dexter,
Whose husband exceedingly vexed her—
For whenever they'd start
He'd let fly a great fart
With a blast that damn nearly unsexed her.

I knew a fair maiden called Heather,
Whose labia were fashioned in leather.
She made a strange noise,
Which attracted the boys,
By flapping the edges together.

———

Once was a young man named Hal,
Who was having a St. Louis gal.
She said: "Oh, you sluggard!"
He said: "You be buggered!
I like to fuck slow, and I shall."

———

A friend of friend's name was Eve,
Who did things you wouldn't believe,
With uncut cucumbers,
And horny young plumbers,
And a dachschund she wants to retrieve!

My trousersnake stands up and cheers
When confronted with boobs in brassieres;
But in charming my cobra,
The bosom with no bra
Can almost reduce it to tears.

———✺———

I could hear the faint buzz of a bee
As it buried its sting deep in me.
Her ass, it was fine,
But you should have seen mine
In the shade of the old apple tree.

———✺———

There was a young lady from Channelview
Whose boyfriend said, "May I explore you?"
She replied to the chap,
"I will draw you a map
Where the others have been to before you."

A woman who lived on a hill,
Had a cunt that could bark, neigh, or trill.
The hunting set hopped her,
Fucked, buggered, then dropped her
When the pitch of her organ went shrill.

———

There was a young man of Hong Kong
Who sported ten inches of prong.
It looked, when erect,
As one would expect—
But when coiled, it did not seem long.

———

There was a young lady named Lottie,
Who had a magnificent body.
And her face was not bad,
Yet she'd never been had,
For her odor was markedly coddy.

Evangeline Alice Du Bois
Committed a dreadful faux pas.
She loosened a stay
In her décolleté,
Exposing her je ne sais quoi.

—◈—

A timid young maiden with grace
Said, "Darling! That's not the right place!"
So he gave her a smack,
And did on her back,
What he couldn't have done face-to-face.

—◈—

There was a young lady called Astor,
Who seldom let any get past her.
One night she got plenty
And finished at twenty.
One imagines that that ought to last her!

Said a man to a maid in Ashanti,
"Can one sniff your privates, or can't he?"
Said she with a grin,
"Sure, stick your nose in!
But presto, please, not too andante."

———∾∾∾———

A virgin emerged from her bath
In a state of righteous wrath.
For she'd been deflowered
When she bent as she showered
'Cause the handle was right in her path.

———∾∾∾———

All was well with the Dowager Duchess
When trapped in the mad rapist's clutches.
'Til he turned on the light,
Took one look, said goodnight,
So she hit him with one of her crutches.

There was a gay Countess of Dufferin,
One night while her husband was coverin',
Just to chaff him a bit,
She said, "You old shit,
I can buy a dildo 'stead of sufferin.'"

—⁓—

In his youth our old friend Boccaccio
Was having a girl on a patio;
When it came to the twat
She wasn't so hot,
But, boy, was she good at fellatio!

—⁓—

Growing tired of her husband's great mass,
A young bride inserted some glass.
The cock of her hubby
Is now short and stubby,
And the wife can piss out of her ass.

There was a young man from Cape Horn,
Who wished he had never been born.
And he wouldn't have been,
If his father had seen
That the tip of the rubber was torn!

———

There was a young Turkish cadet—
And this is the damnedest one yet.
His tool was so long,
And incredibly strong,
He could buttfuck six Greeks *en brochette*.

———

There was a young man from Madras,
Who was stuffing a maid in the grass.
But the tropical sun
Spoiled some of his fun
By singeing the hairs on his ass.

A female magician's best stunt
Was all her spectators could want.
She could reach down and snare
A spectacular hare,
From her perfectly clean-shaven cunt!

There was an old warden of Wadham, he
Was very much given to sodomy.
But he shyly confessed,
"I like tongue-fucking best.
God bless my soul, ain't it odd of me?"

A book and a jug and a dame,
And a nice cozy nook for the same.
"And I don't care a damn,"
Said Omar Khayyám,
"What you say. It's a great little game."

Oh, Shakespeare's love life, 'twould seem,
Was something not quite on the beam.
Too lazy to fuck,
Not wanting to suck,
He preferred *A Midsummer Night's Dream*.

———

Once Shakespeare awoke with a scream,
His underclothes dripping with cream.
'Twas just a commission
Of nocturnal emission
Which he dubbed, "A Mid-Slumber Night's Stream."

———

On Halloween a young girl from the coast
Was screwed in the park by a ghost.
At the height of orgasm
This pale ectoplasm
Cried, "I think I can feel it—almost."

There was a young rent boy called Taylor,
Who seduced a respectable sailor.
When they put him in jail
He settled the bail
By doing the same to the jailor.

—⟋⟍—

A tidy young girl from Berlin
Chose to eke out a living through sin.
Although she loved fucking,
She much preferred sucking,
And wiped off the pricks with her chin.

—⟋⟍—

As the elevator car left our floor,
Big Sue caught her chest in the door.
She yelled a good deal,
But had they been real,
She'd have yelled considerably more.

There was a young lady of Cambridge,
Whose conduct was odd at her marriage.
She proceeded on skates
To the parish church gates,
While her friends followed on in a carriage.

—∞—

A reckless young woman from France
Had no qualms about taking a chance,
But considered it crude
To get screwed in the nude,
So she always went home with damp pants.

—∞—

There was a young fellow named Pete,
Who pranced as he walked down the street.
He wore shoes of bright red
And playfully said,
"I may not be thtrong, but I'm thweet."

There was a young fellow named Hatch,
Who thought that he'd made a great catch.
His inducement to flirt,
Was a wee mini-skirt,
But, alas, she'd a wee mini-snatch.

———

A pretty wife dwelling in Tours
Asked much of her faithful amour.
But her husband said, "No!
On I just cannot go!
My testes are dragging the floor."

———

If Leo your own birthday marks,
You will lust until forty, when starts
A new pleasure in stamps,
Boy scouts, and their camps,
And groping nude statues in parks.

Said the hunter of game to Miss Granger,
"To the feeling of fear I'm no stranger.
I respect the big cat
In his wild habitat,
But a pussy that small is no danger."

———

There was a young novice of Chichester,
Whose form made the saints in their niches stir.
One morning at prayer,
Her bosom quite fair,
Made the bishop of Chichester's britches stir.

———

An astronomer slept in the sun,
Then woke with his fly quite undone.
He remarked, with a smile,
"Hoorah! A sundial!
And it's now a quarter past one."

A copper from Old Clapham Junction,
Whose organ had long ceased to function,
Deceived his dear wife
For the rest of her life
With the aid of his constable's truncheon.

—∞∞—

There once was a cowboy named Fred,
Went to Texas in search of good head.
He went first to Dallas,
And found Pussy Palace,
And settled for that place instead!

—∞∞—

At her husband's relentless insisting,
She posted an S&M listing,
Having just one restriction
Regarding the friction,
That disallowed vaginal fisting.

A lascivious parson named Wings
Liked to talk of loose women and things.
But his secret desire
Was a boy in the choir
With a bottom like jelly on springs.

———

There was a fair maiden whose joys
Were achieved with remarkable poise.
She would reach her orgasm
With scarcely a spasm,
And could fart without making a noise.

———

'Twas a prissy young missy named Laura,
Who was had by a lad from Kenora,
But the fit was so tight
That, though try as he might,
He just couldn't do anything more-a.

A lady was once heard to weep,
"My figure no more I can keep.
It's my husband's demand
For a tit in each hand,
And the bastard will walk in his sleep!"

———

There was a young virgin called Flynn—
Who thought fornication a sin,
But when she was tight,
It seemed quite all right,
So everyone filled her with gin.

———

There once was a fellow named Brink,
Who possessed an extremely tart dink.
To sweeten it some,
He soaked it in rum.
Now he's driven his girlfriend to drink.

Cried the virgin who lay on her back,
"Oh Lord, won't you cut me some slack!
This guy's hung like a horse,
And he wants intercourse,
But I fear he'll get wedged in my crack."

———

As he lay in his bath, mused Lord Ming:
"Oh, Vimy! What memories you bring—
That gorgeous young trooper ...
Er ... No! ... Gladys Cooper!"
"By Gad, sir! That was a near thing!"

———

At his wedding a bridegroom named Crusoe
Was embarrassed to find his prick grew so.
His eager young bride
Pulled him quickly astride
And was screwed while still wearing her trousseau.

There was a young sexual freak,
Who invented a lingual technique.
It drove women frantic,
Made them feel romantic,
And wore all the beard from his cheek.

There was an old farmer named Young,
Who was quite remarkably hung.
When cleaning the stable,
His member was able
To serve as a fork for the dung.

Our ship's captain, nicknamed Old Randy,
Makes advances to any girl handy;
But when shipwrecked a while
On a bleak desert isle,
He made do with Midshipman Sandy.

I hired a housemaid named Nancy—
She does all the cleaning sans panties.
When she picked up the trash,
I noticed her gash,
Now all of her sisters are aunties.

———∽∾∽———

The priests of the temple of Isis
Used to offer up amber and spices,
Then nip round the shrine
And perform sixty-nine
And other unpardonable vices.

———∽∾∽———

There was once a beautiful palace,
By the sea, with a vine-covered trellis.
And where? Up beyond—
Yonder oaks, leafy frond,
Rose a turret, tall, shaped like my phallus.

There was a young maiden from Queens,
Who started to pee in four streams.
A friend poked around,
And a fly-button found,
Tightly wedged in her intimate seams.

———∾∾∾———

A curious mammal's the beaver;
Known often to give men the fever.
A taste to be trying
But there's no damn denying,
It looks to be split by a cleaver!

———∾∾∾———

A hooker of note called Miss Flux
Could command at least two hundred bucks.
But for that she would suck you
And jerk-off and fuck you—
The whole thing was simply deluxe!

A worn-out young hooker from Rome
Was fatigued from her toes to her dome.
Eight soldiers came screwing,
But she said, "Nothing doing;
One of you has to go home!"

—⦿—

An inquisitive virgin named Dora,
Whose boy was beginning to bore her:
"Do you mean birds and bees
Go through antics like these
To provide us with fauna and flora?"

—⦿—

One day at the beach, it was sunny.
Lying down was a curvy beach bunny.
Her swimsuit, cut high,
Revealed lots of thigh,
And I spied just the edge of her cunny.

There was an old maid from Bermuda,
Who shot a marauding intruder.
It was not just her ire
At his lack of attire,
But he reached for her jewels as he screwed her.

———

In Boston a young deb named Brooks
Had a hobby of reading sex books.
She married a Cabot
Who looked like a rabbit,
And deftly lived up to his looks.

———

O, my love's a bonnie red rose,
Newly sprung from her dropped pantyhose.
Her petals bedewed
Arouse me when viewed,
In that fluorescent labial pose.

A young violinist from Rio
Was seducing a lady named Cleo.
As she slipped off her panties
She said, "No andantes;
I want this allegro *con brio*!"

—⟋⟍—

An elderly lecher from York
Had a prick that was dry as a cork.
While attempting to screw,
He split it in two,
And now his poor tool's a fork.

—⟋⟍—

Breathed a tender young man from Australia,
"My darling, please let me unveil ya.
And then, oh my own,
If you'll kindly lie prone,
I'll endeavour, my sweet, to impale ya."

The ex of Miss North Carolina
Has pics of her boobs and vagina.
He wanted a fortune
Obtained by extortion;
He ought to be kicked clear to China.

An astonished young bride in Hong Kong
Found her husband abnormally strong.
She knew about sex
And its heady effects,
But thought thirty-two times might be wrong.

An unusual chap, I should mention,
Has a hair-lined lower intestine.
Though exceedingly fine
In the buttfucking line,
It's notoriously poor for digestin'.

The tool of a fellow called Randall
Shot sparks like a fine Roman candle.
His glorious stand
Produced colors quite grand,
But the girls found him too hot to handle.

There was a young fellow named Peach,
Who fell fast asleep on the beach.
His dreams of nude women
Had his proud organ brimming,
And squirting on all within reach.

A curious thing, the vagina;
Besides being a lovely recliner,
It has lips that don't talk,
And goes "squish" when you walk,
But I can't think of anything finer!

There were two rampant men of Jahore,
Who buttfucked and banged the same whore.
But the partition split,
And both semen and shit
Leaked out in a gush on the floor.

—◈—

There was a young girl who was rare—
Her body was covered in hair.
It was really quite fun
To probe with one's gun,
For the target might be anywhere.

—◈—

She looked terribly fragile and small,
As she stood with her back to the wall.
But she opened her sluices,
And let out her juices,
And bloody near flooded the hall!

There was a young maid named McDuff
With a lovely luxuriant muff.
In his haste to get in her,
One eager beginner
Lost both of his balls in the rough.

———〰———

A tourist in Rome, from South Bend,
Decried sodomy to an old friend.
Leered a visiting Bulgar,
"You may say it's vulgar,
But you will find it's fun, in the end."

———〰———

Jo Mary, a girl who's from Eccles,
A romp with her costs fifty shekels.
For though she was pretty,
It was a great pity
That her muff was all dandruff and freckles.

Two queers who lived in Bombay
Ran into each other one day.
They stood nose to nose,
Then exchanged blows,
And happily went on their way.

—◦◦◦—

A randy young knave from Big Bend
Let a pretty girl play with his end.
She took hold of Rover,
And felt it all over,
And it did what she didn't intend.

—◦◦◦—

Cried the lovely young Molly McFee,
"I'm as chaste as a woman can be!"
But to judge from the guys
Who swarmed her like flies,
That's spelled c-h-a-s-e-d.

There was a young fellow named Dice
Who remarked, "They say bigamy's nice.
Even two is a bore,
I prefer three or four,
For the plural of spouse—it is spice."

There once was a creature from space,
Who had ass where he should have had face.
An eye was an ear,
Balls hung from the rear,
But his willy was in the right place.

There once was a lady from Maine,
Who when fucked would experience pain.
She said to her man,
"Now, listen up, Dan,
Please get out of my rectal drain."

I supposed I just might be perturbed,
If the length was a measly third
Of the width through the middle,
So I'd rather not fiddle
With your highly compressed little bird.

There once was a fellow who was regal,
He decided to buttfuck a beagle,
But just as he came,
A voice called his name,
Saying, "Now me, but you know it's illegal."

A randy young fellow called Reg
Was jerking off under a hedge.
The gardener drew near
With a large pruning shear,
And lopped off the edge of his wedge.

I knew a teenager named Skinner,
Who once took a girl out to dinner.
At a quarter to nine
They sat down to dine.
At a quarter past ten it was in her.
(P.S. The dinner, not Skinner.
Skinner was in her before dinner.)

———

"Her pussy is rated a ten,"
He said with his face in a grin.
"It's firm and it's tight—
An incredible sight;
I want it again and again!"

———

There was once a king who was cute,
But he was troubled by warts on his root.
He put acid on these,
And now when he pees,
He can finger his root like a flute.

A young bride and groom of Australia
Remarked as they joined genitalia:
"Though the system seems odd,
We are thankful that God
Developed the genus *Mammalia*."

A lady by passion deluded
Found a hobo quite drunk and denuded,
And—fit as a fiddle,
And hot for a diddle—
She tied splints to his penis and screwed it.

I love the smell of fresh roses;
It always tickles my nose's
Fancy just right,
Each day and each night,
When you sit on my face striking poses!

There was a young Scot from Dumfries
Who said to his girl, "If you please,
It would give me great joy
If with this you could toy,
Then pay some attention to these."

———

There's a luscious young charmer named Carmen,
Who fucks bums, boxers, and barmen.
Says she, "The elite
Have more brains, but less meat—
I prefer hairy fellows who are men!"

———

Roxanne was a cat burglar's daughter,
Stealing diamonds the way he had taught her.
Having hid the hot rocks,
In a pouch up her box,
She would relish the search if they caught her.

An adventurous lady from Troy
Invented a new kind of joy.
She sugared her muff,
And frosted the fluff,
And then had it sucked by a boy.

———❦———

There once was a man from Manila,
Who lived with five girls in a villa.
When they'd go to bed,
They loved giving head,
'Cause he'd soak it all day in vanilla.

———❦———

There was an old fellow of Lyme,
Who lived with three wives at a time.
When asked, "Why the third?"
He replied, "One's absurd;
And bigamy, sir, is a crime."

There was a young lady of Exeter,
So pretty that men craned their necks at her.
One was even so brave,
As to take out and wave
The distinguishing mark of his sex at her.

―〰―

"I would doubt," said the Bishop of Balham,
"Whether Tennyson ever screwed Hallam.
Such things are best hid.
Let us hope that he did:
'De mortuis nil nisi malum'."

―〰―

There was a young woman called Gloria,
Who was had by Sir Gerald Du Maurier,
By six other men,
Sir Gerald again,
And the band of the Waldorf-Astoria.

"A ripened banana, quite slim,
Is tasty when stuck in," says Jim.
When slipped in the wife,
Just munch for your life,
But suck as you're nearing the rim.

There was a young lady named May,
Who was asked to make love in the hay.
She jumped at the chance
And took off her pants:
She was tickled to try it that way.

There was a young lady of Chester,
Who fell in love with a jester.
Though her breath came out hotly
At the sight of his motley,
It was really his wand that impressed her.

There was a young fellow named Phil,
Who was screwing a girl, as boys will.
She had a girl's knack
Of screwing right back:
The instinct's not easy to kill.

—⚬⚬⚬—

If you're speaking of actions immoral,
Then how about giving the laurel
To doughty Queen Esther,
No three men could best her,
One fore, one aft, and one oral.

—⚬⚬⚬—

There once was an artist called Tensill,
Whose tool was as sharp as a pencil.
He drove through an actress,
The sheet, and the mattress,
And shattered the bedroom utensil.

There was an old abbot most docile,
Who found a remarkable fossil.
He could tell from the bend,
And the wart on the end,
'Twas the peter of Paul the Apostle.

———

There was a young lady named Hopper,
Her long hair was the color of copper;
She went to South Bend
With a gentleman friend—
The rest of the tale is improper.

———

The best pussy, by far, is a young hen—
It's perfectly ripe for a tongue-in.
There's no labial distortions
From a wee-one's contortions;
No distension from fucking hung men.

A modern young lady named Hall
Went out to a birth control ball.
She was carrying pessaries
And other accessories,
But no one approached her at all.

—⁘—

A busty young laundress called Spangle
Had tits tilting up at an angle.
"They may tickle my chin,"
She said, with a grin,
"But at least they avoid any tangle."

—⁘—

A delighted, incredulous bride
Remarked to the groom at her side,
"I never could quite
Believe 'til tonight
Our anatomies would coincide!"

Said Mary, while stroking her clit,
"It's really a nice little slit,
But unlike my behind,
Will I ever find
Someone to fit inside it?"

⟞⟋⟍⟞

A sodomist, fresh out of jail,
Was desperate for some sort of tail.
He griped and he griped,
And then screwed the pipe
Of a van that was marked "Royal Mail."

⟞⟋⟍⟞

A girl called Alice from Dallas
Had yet to experience phallus.
She remained *virgo intacta*,
Because, ipso facto,
No phallus in Dallas fit Alice.

There was a young woman who'd squeal
While every new fellow would kneel,
To revere her small pussy,
As fresh as a sushi,
And to relish the scent of an eel.

I knew a young dentist called Stone
Who saw all his patients alone.
In a fit of depravity
He filled the wrong cavity,
Good Lord! How his practice has grown!

Two innocent ladies from Grimsby
Inquired, "Of what use can our cunts be?
The hole in the middle
Is so we can piddle,
But for what can the rest of the thing be?"

In Hong Kong, a Texan named Lou
Was looking for ladies to screw.
Said the madam, Miss Chang,
After feeling his wang,
"My girls have small cunts, so take two."

———❦———

There was an old man from Tagore,
Whose tool was a foot long—or more.
He supported the thing
In a surgical sling,
To prevent it from scuffing the floor.

———❦———

An astonished young lady named Bissell
Let out a lascivious whistle
When her boyfriend stripped nude.
He remarked, "Though it's crude,
Please observe that it's muscle, not missile!"

An eager young bride, Mrs. Strong,
Thought that passion would last all night long,
And her husband's capacity
Would match her voracity—
But (alas!), it turned out she was wrong.

———

Emily, you're the one that I love,
You sweet little blonde turtle dove.
I don't give a snort
If you are a bit short,
'Cause your pussy's as tight as a glove.

———

There once was a maiden from Thrace
Whose corsets grew too tight to lace.
Her mother said, "Nelly,
There's things in your belly
That never got in through your face."

There once was a man from St. Kit,
Whose ass cheeks were terribly thick.
They had to be parted
Whenever he farted,
And propped wide apart when he shit.

———

There once was a couple I found
Whose sexual control was profound:
When engaged in coition,
They had the ambition
To study the Cantos of Pound.

———

The crotch of a lady from Trenton
Was too tight to make much of a dent in.
The fellows who tried,
Spread the news far and wide,
That she made of a hard-on, a bent one.

An insatiable lady from Spain,
Had multiple sex on the brain.
She liked it again,
And again, and again,
And again, and again, and again.

—✶—

A dancer who came from Darjeeling
Could perform with such sensuous feeling.
There was never a sound
For miles around,
Except buttons as they were hitting the ceiling.

—✶—

There was a new parson of young age,
Tried to grind his betrothed in a carriage.
She said, "No, you horny goose,
Just try self-abuse,
And the other we'll try after marriage."

A gadget collector named Mantz
Brought home a machine made in France.
Now, this is no snow job,
It gives you a blow job,
And stuffs your dick back in your pants.

———

A well-hung young sailor named Bean
Could keep at it like a machine.
As he pummeled their ends,
His society friends
All shouted out, "God Save the Queen!"

———

A girl of dubious nativity
Had an ass of extreme sensitivity.
When she sat on the lap
Of a German or Jap,
She could sense any recent activity.

The Grecians were famed for fine art
And buildings and stonework so smart.
They distinguished with poise
The men from the boys
And used crowbars to keep them apart.

———

A eunuch who hailed from Port Said
Could enjoy a good romp in bed.
Nor could the Sultana
Detect from his manner
That he used a banana instead.

———

There was an old botanist, Pace,
Who grew pussies in a pot at his place.
When they'd ripen, he'd pluck them,
And eat them or fuck them—
They were simpler to grow than to chase.

Said the Cardinal to Mother Superior,
"Your singing is very inferior!"
She, not to be crass,
Did show some real class
She said, "You can kiss my posterior!"

———

There was a young girl named Miss Moore,
Who'd lie on a mat on the floor.
In a manner uncanny,
She'd wriggle her fanny,
And drain your nuts dry to the core.

———

Anthropologists up with the Sioux
Cabled home for two punts, one canoe.
The answer next day,
Said, "Girls on their way,
But what the hell is a panoe?"

There once was a fellow named Scott,
Who thought he was really quite hot.
    Then Suzie dumped him,
    And her new man, he thumped him—
Now a living Scott there is not.

———∿∿∿———

A rascal, far gone in treachery,
Lured maids to their doom with his lechery;
    He invited them in
    For the purpose of sin,
Though he said 'twas to look at his etchery.

———∿∿∿———

There was a young man of Savannah,
Met his end in a curious manner.
    He diddled a hole
    In a telegraph pole,
And electrified his banana.

There was a young lady of Pinner
Whose hubby came home to his dinner;
And guess what he saw
As he opened the door?
The butt of the man who was in her.

———

A languid young man from Racine
Wasn't weaned until nearly sixteen.
He said, "I'll admit
There's no milk in the tit,
But think of the fun it has been."

———

There was a young squaw of Chokdunt
Who had a collapsible cunt.
Though it had many uses,
It made no papooses,
But fitted both giant and runt.

A Newfoundland lad from Placentia,
Was in love to the point of dementia.
But his love didn't burgeon
With this touch-me-not virgin
'Til he screwed her by hand, in absentia.

—∽∾∽—

Beware of Christina. Perhaps
You've been tempted to open her flaps,
And stick Thomas inside.
But her cunt is supplied
With incisors—so watch it, they snaps!

—∽∾∽—

There was a young person called Herman,
Who spoke both falsetto and German.
Behind the blonde hair
There was somebody there
But its sex one could never determine.

A disturbing tale comes from Niger
Of a lady, her donkey, a tiger.
What occurred in the bush
Might have remained hush-hush,
But for the ass print on the face of the tiger.

———

There was a young girl with a bust,
Which aroused a French cavalier's lust.
She was since heard to say,
About midnight, "Touché!
I didn't quite parry that thrust!"

———

Said an awfully innocent siren,
"Young sailors are cute—I must try one!"
She came home in the nude,
Stewed, screwed, and tattooed
With lewd pictures and verses from Byron.

Step 1 says to insert your blade,
Choose a scene. How about Woodland Glade?
Step 2 says divest
Our clothes for the test.
Step 3 says we now can get laid!

———

"It's dull in Duluth, Minnesota.
Of spunk there is not an iota,"
Complained Alice to Joe,
Who tried not to show
That he yawned as he poked with his bloater.

———

A singular lady called Grace
Had eyes in a very strange place.
She could sit on the hole
Of a mouse or a mole
And stare the beast straight in the face.

The ants in the pants of Miss Morse
Would dance with such passion and force.
When in southern France,
She left off her pants,
And let nature take its own course.

———

It's recorded that Emperor Titius
Had a preference for pleasures most vicious.
He took two of his nieces
And fucked them to pieces,
And thought it completely delicious.

———

There was a young lady name Janis,
Who said, "What a wonder my fan is.
If I draw the lips back,
I've a hole, not a crack
Into which pricks can seemingly vanish."

Said the newlyweds staying near Whiteley,
"We turn out the electric light nightly.
It's best to embark
Upon sex in the dark;
The look of the thing's so unsightly."

The boy to his girl proudly crows,
"Here's something that you don't have, Rose."
"That's true," said the miss,
"But just look at this.
And with this, I can get lots of those."

There was a young lady from Butte
Obsessed with a man of repute.
She spent many an hour
Peeking in at his shower
While tuning the strings of her lute.

A vice both obscure and unsavory
Kept the Bishop of Chester in slavery.
Amid terrible howls
He deflowered young owls
In a crypt fitted out as an aviary.

———∽∽∽———

Said an urgent young sailor called Micky,
As his girl eyed his stiff, throbbing dicky,
"Pet, my leave's almost done,
And I need some good fun—
Bend over, and I'll slip you a quickie."

———∽∽∽———

There was once an effeminate Ottoman;
For the fair sex, I fear, he was not a man.
He was all up in arms
Against feminine charms:
"Quite frankly," he said, "I'm a bottom man."

There was a young man of Bengal,
Who went to a fancy-dress ball.
Just for a stunt,
He dressed up as a cunt
And was had by a dog in the hall.

The Grenadiers are very strange bods.
While marching the park, formed in squads,
They saw two nude statues
From three-quarter rear views,
Which noticeably stiffened their rods.

Some pussies are rather deplorable,
While others are very adorable;
But while this is true,
From my point of view,
All pussies are surely explorable!

There was an old widower, Doyle,
Who wrapped up his wife in tin foil.
He thought it would please her,
To stay in the freezer,
And, anyway, outside she'd spoil.

—◦◦◦—

"It's no use," said Lady Maude Hoare,
"I can't concentrate anymore.
You're all in a sweat,
And the sheets are quite wet,
And just look at the time: half-past four!"

—◦◦◦—

Oh, you Angel, I love to get flashed;
Yes, hell yes, whether sober or smashed;
When you sit, not too far,
And your legs drift ajar,
My poor eyeballs bug out, unabashed!

"It is a delight here," said old Mr. Spanks,
"To walk up the green river banks.
One time, in the grass
I stepped on an ass,
And heard a young girl murmur, 'Thanks!'"

———

Fuck me quick, fuck me deep, fuck me oft,
In the bog, in the bath, in the loft,
Up my ass, up my cunt,
From behind, from in front,
With your best, stiffest stand, nothing soft.

———

A notorious whore named Miss Hearst
In the weakness of men is well-versed;
Reads a sign over the head
Of her well-rumpled bed:
"The customer always comes first."

Cold weather, when it's in the minuses,
Is hell on a guy's aging sinuses;
If you need a spot
To keep your nose hot,
A twat's the best place; at least Dinah's is.

———

A horny young fellow called Rick
Liked to feel a girl's hand on his prick.
He taught them to fool
With his tumescent tool,
'Til his well-polished member was sick.

———

There was a young fellow called Dirk
Who dozed off one day after work.
He woke with a scream
When he had a wet dream,
And polished it off with a jerk.

A widow whose singular vice
Was to keep her late husband on ice.
Said, "It's been hard since I lost him—
I'll never defrost him!"
(Cold comfort, but cheap at the price.)

—ഗഗ—

A prudish young maiden from Florence
Wrote anti-sex pamphlets in torrents,
'Til a Spanish grandee
Got her hot with his knee,
And she burned all her works with abhorrence.

—ഗഗ—

Alas, the poor Duchess of Kent!
Her cunt is amazingly bent.
The poor thing doth stammer,
"I need a sledgehammer
To pound a man into my vent!"

While Titian was mixing rose madder,
His model reclined on a ladder.
Her position, to Titian,
Suggested coition,
So he leapt up the ladder and had her.

———∞———

There was a young lady from Hadham
Very fond of the primitive Adam.
Whatever the name
Of the men on the game
The madam from Hadham had had 'em.

———∞———

There once was a young girl from Norway,
Who hung by her feet from the doorway;
Which worked out quite well,
'Cause when you rang her bell,
It actually turned out to be foreplay!

The hell with this shit.
I must be a twit.
Limericks are written,
With blood, sweat, an' spittin'.
I can rhyme but can't get the rhythm right so I quit.

———∾———

There once was a lad named Tristan
Whose beer that he ordered was pissed in
He said "I don't think,"
As he spat out his drink,
"On the menu that this one's existin.'"

———∾———

A man with the name Screwy Dick
Was born with a long, spiral prick.
His life was a hunt
For a true spiral cunt,
That would not give his willy a crick.

THE SAGA OF EVA AND KATE

Before they were finally blessed
Young Eva said, "Wait, here's a test.
Before I agree
To be wedded to thee
Will you strip to your boxers and vest?"

"And you," she said pointing at Stan,
The lovelorn, besotted best man.
When both of the guys
Had stripped naked (unwise)
Eva cried, "How pathetic!" and ran.

Poor Timothy cried as his mate
Said, "I do" and "I will" to young Kate.
"But, I love you, dear Stan,"
Said young Tim, the best man.
"Have I left it, dear Stanley, too late?"

"Oh, Timothy, why didn't you say
So," said Stanley, "Before my big day?
No, it isn't too late;
I'm so sorry, dear Kate,
But with Tim I shall now go away."

Now Eva (who fled from the church)
And Kate (who was left in the lurch)
Met up for a rabbit
As oft is the habit
Of girlies when men they besmirch.

"He this" and "He that" and "I shouldn't;
But to tell you the truth, dear, he couldn't."
"He couldn't?" "Well, no."
"Did you put on a show?"
"No, he's teensy and I said I wouldn't."

What now of poor Eva and Kate
In their search for a regular mate?
Well they seemed pretty buoyant
As off to Claire Voyant
They went to learn more of their fate.

"I see," said mysterious Claire,
As she juggled her balls in the air,
"That young Eva will meet
Maybe Roger or Pete
And that Kate will wed Matthew, I swear."

"What absolute garbage!" they said,
As they snatched back their money and fled.
"There must be some men
Who rate ten out of ten,"
Said young Kate as to Bristol they sped.

(Why Bristol? I haven't a clue;
I guess London or Glasgow would do;
Even Llanfairpwllgwyn
Or Caernarvon wherein
They could find them a Druid or two.)

And lo! As onward they sped,
They encountered a guy, name of Fred
And his brother called Joe,
Both good-looking, and so
They decided right then to get wed.

Though Eva, Kate, Joseph, and Fred
In a Bristol hotel shared a bed,
They eschewed any hanky
And similar panky
Last night (so the chambermaid said).

This morning they all woke at eight.
"Oh, good heavens; the wedding!" said Kate.
"It's at quarter to one,"
Replied Eva, "Now run
To the bathroom or else we'll be late."

So meanwhile the guys ordered food
And champagne to help get in the mood.
Then waited for hours
While the girls took their showers
As on oysters they furtively chewed.

At last Kate and Eva emerged.
Though the bridegrooms' testosterone surged
At the sight. "Now stop
That," said Eva, "Chop chop—
Get a move on and hurry!" she urged.

We cut to the church of St. Clyde,
Where the guys are so nervous inside,
That they jump out their skins
As the organ begins
A fortissimo "Here Comes the Bride."

Old Morgan the organ enjoys
All the pedals and stops he employs;
But he's deaf, which explains
The fortissimo strains
And the simply cacophonous noise.

Not only can Morgan not hear
He instills congregational fear
As he thumps out cantatas,
Sonatas, toccatas,
And fugues with a devilish leer.

Quite frankly, old Morgan is mad
And he's losing his marbles a tad;
But the vicar daren't say
To him, "Call it a day,"
For old Morgan, you see, is his dad.

But back once again to St. Clyde
And the deafening "Here Comes the Bride,"
As the ultimate mordant,
Sforzando, discordant,
Fortissimo chords now subside.

The bridegrooms are quaking in fear,
As the brides, Kate and Eva, appear
Waving brightly at Morgan
Slumped over his organ
Exhausted from playing, it's clear.

The vicar emerges from under
The altar, his features like thunder,
And says to the lovers
('Fore Morgan recovers)
"Let no man dare put you asunder."

"That's it? I'm now wed?" says young Kate.
"But, of course," says the vicar. "But wait."
She replies, "If I'm wed
Am I married to Fred
Or is Joseph my nuptial mate?"

"It's Eva I've married," says Joe.
"It bloody well isn't, you know;
I'm wedded to Fred,"
Replies Eva, "instead."
To which Freddie says, "Katie, let's go!"

The vicar is heard to remark,
"Stop this bickering children." But hark!
They've awakened old Morgan
Now poised o'er his organ—
Oh, God; now he's murdering Bach.

It seems that a harlot in Natchez
Was blessed from birth with two snatches.
With half her appliance,
She services clients.
The other is stuffed with book matches.

———

There once was a nun from Siberia,
Who was born with a virgin interior.
Until a young monk,
Jumped into her bunk,
And now she's a mother superior.

———

There was a young student named Jones,
Who reduced all maidens to groans
By his wonderful knowledge
Acquired in college
Of nineteen erogenous zones.

A businesslike harlot named Draper
Once tried an unusual caper.
What made it so nice,
Was you got it half-price,
If you brought in her ad from the paper.

—◦◦◦—

When Smith caught his tool in some gears
They grafted on skin from his ears.
And now the poor guy
Can hear through his fly,
But screwing just bores him to tears.

—◦◦◦—

There once was a faddist of Devon
Who said "I have raped only seven
Young women to date,
But soon it'll be eight
And shortly thereafter eleven."

A young airline stewardess, May,
Has achieved the ultimate lay.
She was screwed without quittin'
From New York to Britain.
It's clear that she's come a long way.

A horny young sailor named Clark
Once picked up a slut in a park.
She was ugly and crude
And a horror when nude,
But good for a spell in the dark.

There once was a fellow named Mark,
Who spread a girl's legs in the dark.
He said, "Now by thunder,
A natural wonder—
I declare this a national park."

There once was a man from Osaka,
Who decided to screw his alpaca.
He started quite normal,
But when he tried oral,
The beastie bit off his left knacker.

Other Ulysses Press Books

The Big Ass Book of Jokes
Rudy A. Swale, $14.95
The thousands of jokes in this huge volume range from clean enough to tell at work to too off-color for corporate e-mail.

Blonde Walks into a Bar: The 4,000 Most Hilarious, Gut-Busting Gags, One-Liners and Jokes
Jonathan Swan, $14.95
Unapologetically funny and irreverent, this book holds nothing back as it delivers laugh after laugh.

The Dirtiest, Most Politically Incorrect Jokes Ever
Allan Pease, $12.95
This book is packed with no-holds-barred gags for those who are fed up with others telling them what to say, how to think, and what is allowed to be funny.

The Ginormous Book of Dirty Jokes: Over 1000 Sick, Filthy and X-Rated Jokes
Rudy A. Swale, $12.95
This masterpeice offers the biggest, baddest, badassest collection of off-color quips.

Man Walks into a Bar: Over 6,000 of the Most Hilarious Jokes, Funniest Insults and Gut-Busting One-Liners
Stephen Arnott & Mike Haskins, $14.95
This book is packed full of quick and easy jokes that are as simple to remember and repeat as they are funny.

The Sassy Bitch's Book of Dirty Jokes
Katie Reynolds, $10.95
Features outrageous one-liners, stories, and jokes on everything from romance and dirty talk to penis size and between-the-sheets mishaps.

Seriously Sick Jokes: The Most Disgusting, Filthy, Offensive Jokes from the Vile, Obscene, Disturbed Minds of b3ta.com
Compiled by Rob Manuel, $10.95
Seriously Sick Jokes is a lewd, crude, and absolutely filthy collection that will have readers cringing between bouts of uncontrollable laughter.

The Ultimate Book of Blonde, Brunette and Redhead Jokes
James Buffington, $12.95
An equal-opportunity offender, this hilarious collection of shamelessly funny jokes spares no one as it rips on less-than-brilliant blondes, uptight brunettes, and hot-tempered redheads.

The Ultimate Dirty Joke Book
Mike Oxbent & Harry P. Ness, $11.95
This joke collection holds back nothing and guarantees outrageous laughs.

To order these books call 800-377-2542 or 510-601-8301, fax 510-601-8307, e-mail ulysses@ulyssespress.com, or write to Ulysses Press, P.O. Box 3440, Berkeley, CA 94703. All retail orders are shipped free of charge. California residents must include sales tax. Allow two to three weeks for delivery.